# PRE-WAR 1619–1819
## Seeds of War Sown Early!

I have been uprooted from my homeland... Africa. After a horrible journey across the sea in the nasty hold of a ship, here I am on the shores of a strange and fearful land, at the hands of a white-skinned and cruel people. They say I am their slave, that they can buy and sell me at will. Surely no good can come from such an idea. —**Ella, August 1619, Jamestown, VA**

I is the Infant, from the arms
Of its fond mother torn,
And at a public auction sold
With horses, cows, and corn.

Z is a Zealous man, sincere,
Faithful, and just, and true;
An earnest pleader for the slave—
Will you not be so too?

**We declare slavery illegal.** —Rhode Island, 1652

**Slaves are hereby declared "real estate."** —State of Virginia, 1705

I have frequently seen [slaves] whipt to that degree that large pieces of their skin have been hanging down their backs, yet I never observed one of them to shed a tear. —**John Brickell**

For months and months at a time we weren't allowed off the farm. Sometimes we would get as far as the gate and peep over. We were told that if we got outside the Padirollers would get us. —**Uriah Bennett**, slave

I haven't anything to say against slavery. My old folks put my clothes on me...they gave me shoes and stockings and put them on me when I was a little boy. I loved them, and I can't go against them in anything. There were things I did not like about slavery on some plantations, whuppin' and sellin' parents and children from each other, but I haven't much to say. I was treated good. —**Samuel Riddick**

Slaves bring the judgment of Heaven on a country. —**George Mason**

I's just follow the finger. The white man point his finger and I follow it and do. —**Cuffee**, slave

In 1776 Thomas Jefferson signed the Declaration of Independence, which states "all men are created equal." Jefferson was a slave owner.

I didn't come to America to get along with other people from all over and from other states. What do I care about them? I came for opportunity for me and my family. I'm all for fast progress, and bigger cities, and more work. What do I have in common with those hick farmers in the South—nothing. To the Devil with them! —**blacksmith, Rhode Island**

I was an early victim of slave trading. I was born in Benin, in what is now Nigeria, in 1745. At age 11, I was kidnapped from my family and sold into slavery. Later I was sold again to traders and chained on a slave ship bound for America. I was sold to a Virginia planter, and then to a British naval officer, and finally to a Philadelphia merchant who gave me the chance to buy my freedom. I also worked to bring an end to the slave trade. As a ship's steward, I traveled widely. In 1791, I wrote my autobiography. —**Gustavus Vassa**

Laws, I gots to be up at dawn's crack with the baby to head to the fields. That sun sho is hot. We gots to pick fast today. Massa says is back-breakin' work. It's just one row after another. Gots to stop to nurse the baby as I can, but so the 'seer can't see me. —**Lizzie**, 17, plantation slave

**Eli Whitney invents the cotton gin, 1793.**

Eli Whitney's invention of the cotton gin made it possible for farmers to make more money and harvest more cotton each year. But it also meant farmers needed more workers. So, they bought slaves from Africa to tend their fields. The cotton gin revolutionized farming...and slavery.

1619...1st slaves to America land in Virginia...1652...Rhode Island declares slavery illegal...1688...1st public protest of slave trade in Pennsylvania...1700

1829...A free black, David Walker, publishes an essay which encourages slaves to revolt. As a result, most southern states make it illegal to teach slaves to read and write...1830...Anti-Slavery Movement begins...1831...Maria Stewart is the first

# 1820–1860 Antebellum = "Before the War"

**The Fugitive Slave Act of 1793 demands the return of runaway slaves.**

abolitionist: person who worked to do away with slavery

*Slavery is a covenant with death and an agreement with hell.*—abolitionist **William Lloyd Garrison**, *The Liberator*, Boston

I don't know why some people can't understand the unity of the South. We have our own identity and traditions. Cotton is my crop and I need my slaves to make a successful living. If those darn Yankees came down here they'd see it's a lot of hot, hard hand-labor, no machine to magically get our crop in and meet the worldwide demand for cotton. Cotton is King, after all!—**plantation owner**, South Carolina

Some people say "The South was built on the backs of blacks."

## COTTON IS KING!

Antislavery newspapers began in 1821 with white editor Benjamin Lundy's *Genius of Universal Emancipation*. It had six subscribers.

It's like this: they's good massas and bad massas. Most white folks not slaves, but be about as po' as we slaves are! My plantation family's good to me.—**slave cook**, Louisiana

Reveille is a bugle call that was used to wake up sleeping soldiers at sunrise. During the Civil War, the call was sounded between 4:45-6:00 in the morning! When the last note played, the flag was raised, a gunshot was fired, and the soldiers had to be dressed and ready for roll call.

Slavery was sometimes called a "necessary evil" or the "peculiar institution."

A plot that involved 9,000 blacks, led by free black Denmark Vesey, was exposed in Charleston, South Carolina in 1822. Vesey and 36 others were executed.

I can't believe a man like that can be President of these United States! Andrew Jackson is nothing but a common man. Newspapers call him a "barbarian," "half-wit," and "tyrant," and I must say, I agree with them. The people got what they wanted, I guess…a low-class man running this whole nation!—**U.S. citizen**, 1828

Only one of every 20 Northerners was an active abolitionist.

I didn't have to be told that if a slave struck his master it meant death. Freeborn in North Carolina, but the son of a slave father, I knew slavery firsthand. My hatred of slavery drove me to Boston, where I sold old clothes and subscriptions to the *Freedom's Journal*. I burned to deliver my own message and in 1829 published my pamphlet, *Walker's Appeal.*—**David Walker**

In 1831, slave Nat Turner led 70 blacks in a revolt that slaughtered 57 men, women, and children in rural Southampton County, Virginia. Troops rushed in to put down the uprising and killed over one hundred blacks—the innocent as well as the insurrectionists—in a savage massacre. Wild rumors and alarms swept through the South—could this happen again?!—**newspaperman**, North Carolina

I didn't know I was a slave until I found out I couldn't do the things I wanted.—Edmund, Georgia

I bet that was a shock!

…Virginia declares slaves are "property"…New York puts runaway slaves to death…1725…Virginia grants slaves right to form own church…1739…Slave black woman to lecture against slavery…William Lloyd Garrison publishes the first edition of the newspaper, Liberator, which called for emancipation of slaves…Nat Turner leads a slave rebellion in Southampton, Virginia…1833…The American and

# THE STUDENT'S CIVIL WAR
## 150TH ANNIVERSARY EDITION • 1861-1865

# CIVIL WAR TRIVIA

*It's all gone with the wind!*

*oh, I wish I was in the land of cotton...*

**True Facts, Tall Tales, Fascinating Folklore, Stories, Songs**

by Carole Marsh

---

*Southerners were polite in calling slavery a "necessary evil." I call slavery a "positive good." I stand by what I said in Congress—slavery is good for blacks!*—**John C. Calhoun**, South Carolina senator, 1837

Boo! Boo!

*I was born a slave. I worked long and hard for my master 22 years. I finally ran away, and been hiding in a small space in my grandmother's attic for seven years. I'm trying to get to the North and gain my freedom. I finally have my chance. A boat is going to take me there tonight. Perhaps by morning, I'll be free!—* **Harriet Jacobs**, North Carolina

### How Come?

When I was born I was black.
When I grew up I was black.
When I'm sick I'm black.
When I go out into the sun I'm black.
When I die I'll be black.

But you:
When you were born you were pink.
When you grow up you are white.
When you get sick you are green.
When you go out in the sun you are red.
When you go out in the cold you are blue.
When you die you turn purple.
And you call me colored?

### $50 Reward!

Ranaway from the Subscriber, living in the county of Edgecombe, NC, about eight miles north of Tarborough, on the 24th of August last, a negro fellow named Washington, about 24 years of age, 5 feet and 8 or 10 inches high, dark complexion, stout built, and an excellent field hand, no particular marks about him recollected.

*Maybe he's on the railroad?*

**sesquicentennial:** (noun) [ses-kwi-sen-ten-ee-uhl] a 150th anniversary or its celebration

### Runaways Held in the New Bern, NC, Jail

Two New Negro Men, the one named Joe, about 45 years of age...much wrinkled in the face, and speaks bad English. The other is a young fellow...speaks better English than Joe, whom he says is his father, has a large scar on the fleshy part of his left arm.... They have nothing with them but an old Negro cloth jacket and an old blue sailor's jacket without sleeves. Also...a Negro named Jack, about 23 years of age...of a thin visage, bleareyed...has six rings of his country marks around his neck, his ears are full of holes.

*I was born on a plantation near Fayetteville, North Carolina, and I belonged to J.B. Smith. He owned about 30 slaves. When a slave was no good, he was put on the auction block in Fayetteville and sold.*
—Sarah Louise Augustus

*What man can make, man can unmake.—* **Frederick Douglass**, abolitionist

---

rebellion in South Carolina; 44 slaves killed...1777...Vermont outlaws slavery...1783...Massachusetts outlaws slavery...1792...Kentucky joins Union as slave

the Female Anti-Slavery Societies are formed in Philadelphia...1833...Oberlin College is the first coed college founded to educate African Americans...1837...The first Anti-Slavery Convention of American Women is held in New

Copyright Year of Our Lord 2010
Carole Marsh/Gallopade International/Peachtree City, GA

*I thought it was the Year of the Tiger.*
*No, that was last year.*  *Oh.*

Permission is hereby granted to the individual purchaser or classroom teacher to reproduce materials in this book for individual or classroom use only. Reproduction of these materials for an entire school or school system is strictly prohibited.
No part of this publication may be reproduced, stored in or introduced into a retrieval system, or transmitted, in any form or by any means (electronic, mechanical, photocopying, recording, or otherwise) without the prior written permission of the publisher of this book.

It takes an army to do a book. Here's ours:

### HEADQUARTERS
Gen. Michele Yother, Gen. Mike Longmeyer, Master Sergeant Cowboy Pilot Bob Longmeyer
Indispensible Right Hand (Wo)man: Nancy "You Gotta Have" Hart

*All you really need is heart, you know.*  *I know.*

### CIVIL WAR CENTRAL
Chief Wrangler: Paige Muh
Sergeant at Art Arms: John Hanson
Scribes, First Class: Whitney Akin, Janice Baker, Sherri Smith Brown
(Battle) Field Artists: Vicki DeJoy, Corie Ferguson, Yvonne Ford, Randolyn Friedlander, Jessica Talley
Erstwhile Intern: Emily Kimbell

*John's relative walked home from the Civil War.*
*Oh, I thought he drove a Volkswagon.*

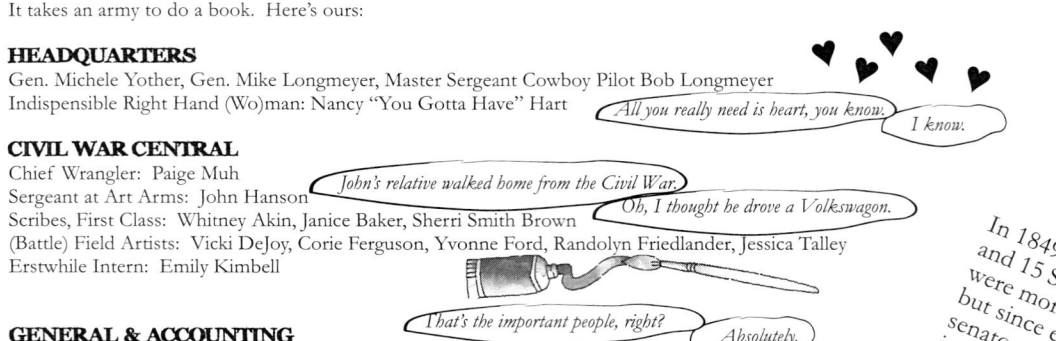

In 1849, there were 15 Northern and 15 Southern states. There were more people in the North, but since each state had 2 senators, in the Senate there was a "stalemate" at that time for any effort to pass laws.

### GENERAL & ACCOUNTING
Muster Masters: Marcie Comeau, Cindy Green, Bri Roden

*That's the important people, right?*  *Absolutely.*

### SALES
*War bonds, right?*  *Sure, wanna buy some?*  *Yeah, my old Confederate currency ok?*

Melessa Hill, Pam Morris, Gina Vranesevich, Lori White, Valerie Curry, Jennifer Johnson
Hallelujah Chorus: Denise Morris

### MARKETING MILITIA
Head of the One-Million-Man E-mail March: Camille Chasteen
Linda Metoyer, Mark Dean, Tammy Weeks, Jennifer Kelly, Justin Badger

*I hate stale things!*

### PRODUCTION & FULFILLMENT
Colonel James Barnard
Dave Guerrero, Pernell Arnold, Kathy Morgan, Jeff Jerabeck

*I need fulfilling.*  *You always do.*

*I remember all the bricklayers; they all was colored... The men that plastered the City Hall outside and put those columns up in the front...they was slaves, mos' all the fine work...was done by slaves. They called 'em artisans. None of 'em could read, but give 'em any plan an' they could foller it to the las' line.* —**John H. Jackson**

### SPECIAL UNIT
Hair and Makeup: Christina Yother
Dance and Funny Faces: Grant Yother
Cheerleader: Avery Longmeyer
PT, Boot Camp, and Gymastics: Ella Longmeyer
Best Boy: Evan "Da? Da?!" Longmeyer

*I could use a makeover.*  *Ya think?*
*My kinda guy!*
*Cute legs!*  *Whata sweetheart!*
*I thought he was the key grip.*  *That, too.*

Private First Class: CAROLE MARSH

*Shouldn't she go up at the top?*  *It's safer down here...out of the line of fire.*  *I'm just sayin'...*

*It took us as long as the war to get done!*

Carole Marsh Civil War and Other Sassy Books for Young Readers are available from your favorite school supply or teacher store, almost all of America's fine museum and park stores, at lovely bookstores everywhere, or if all else fails, direct from www.gallopade.com, or call 1-800-536-2GET (that's 2438), extension 11, Miss Cindy.

We have referred to a few of our favorite Internet and social media sites throughout this book. All trademarks are registered, and belong to their respective owners—none of whom sponsored nor endorsed this book, nor are affiliated with Gallopade International/Carole Marsh Books.

For further information, trade terms, rights sales, good recipes, advice, and more, please contact:
GALLOPADE INTERNATIONAL
6000 Shakerag Hill
Suite 314
Peachtree City, Georgia
30269

*You mean like when the wife stood on the hill and waved her hankie welcoming her Johnny home from the war?*  *The very same!*
*That's in the South, right?*  *Yes.*  *They made up that town name, right?*  *Probably.*

See our bibliography and more at
www.studentscivilwar.com

*I had to try to put an end to this political battle! When the territory of California applied to join the Union in 1849—as a free state—the U.S. had half free and half slave states. To stop this madness, I introduced a bill that would let California be a free state. However, my Compromise of 1850 also said that any new state could choose to be free or slave based on "popular sovereignty", or what the people wanted. After all, a state should have the right to decide what it wants to be, right? My bill passed, but alas, it was only a temporary solution.*—Senator **Henry Clay**, Kentucky

state...1793...The Fugitive Slave Act forces return of runaway slaves...Eli Whitney invents the cotton gin...1796...Tennessee joins Union as slave state...1800

York...1839...Joseph Cinque leads a successful revolt on the slave ship, Amistad...1850...Congress passes the Fugitive Slave Act requiring captured runaway slaves to be returned to their owners. Whites now hunt slaves for profit...

# A Word from the Author

There's a song that goes *"War! What's it all about? Absolutely nothing!"*

However war is usually about *something*. As you know, the Revolutionary War was all about America wrenching herself away from the final grasp of her mother country of England. It was a war to secure freedom, a new nation, and a new way of life. Later, no one looked back and said, "Hey, maybe we shouldn't have fought that war."

Close to a hundred years after America's founding, people were restless. America was now about a lot of ways of life, many quite different from the others. You might be a plantation owner using slave labor to grow your cotton crop. You might be a mountain woman still living in the wilds of Appalachia. You could be a president trying to run the still new, young, ambitious, and sometimes, even cantankerous and disagreeable country.

Two of the major disagreements of the mid-1800s were slavery and states' rights versus federal rights. Some folks said that they could not survive without slave labor, that they were good to their slaves, and that slavery was now a necessary and permanent part of American life. Others said slavery was wrong and that there was no reason any human being should be owned by another. After all, wasn't America about freedom for all people?

Some Americans thought that states should be able to make their own decisions without so much interference from the federal government in Washington. (Sound familiar?) Other Americans insisted that's what Washington and the federal government were for: to keep all states fair and equal and to solve disputes.

You could say that lanky, teenage America had major growing pains! But America was no longer a "kid." America was at a serious crossroads. Would Americans fight their fellow Americans over these issues? Could such disagreements be resolved by talking, cooperation, compromise, and change? Or would we go to war?

What a curious turn of events—to believe you had to fight your fellow countrymen to the death! Wasn't there any other way? As we know today, getting along and solving problems is much better than going to war. Sometimes, if you are under attack, you may feel you have no choice but to go to war to defend your nation, or to defend others.

Let's just say it was complicated. By the spring of 1861, Americans were actually talking about going to war. They made it sound necessary, even exciting. Many believed it would be a quick war—with their side winning, naturally!

Of course, it didn't happen that way. It was a long war—four years—with terrible tragedies. Slavery was ended. But not before most people "took sides" and fought face-to-face, often against people they knew or were related to, until no one any longer felt that war was a good thing, not even a so-called "necessary" war.

What eventually led to war was a long, drawn out, complex, contradictory set of circumstances, actions, misunderstandings, and oversights. Could we have ended slavery and preserved the union—without war? Think about this, for it may be your job to assess, decide, act or not act, or argue for or against some similar situation one day!

As you read, imagine being that person at that time, in that place during that event. How would you feel, what would you do, how would you change? Today, could we possibly still "stumble" into such a long war? Would around-the-clock news make a difference? Would gathering those who disagree around a table and negotiating work? Diplomacy? The Civil War contains a world of wondering!

What was the American Civil War about? What did it mean? Was there another way? Was it fun, exciting? Was it fair? Who won? Who lost? What would you have done? What do you think?

Why does it matter what *you* think? Because in the absence of diplomacy, cooperation, collaboration, compromise, understanding, honor, and integrity, it is war, not peace, that always looms on our horizon. The past was in their hands. The future is in yours.

*Carole Marsh*
Shakerag Hill
Peachtree City, Georgia

Reader,

After you read this book, you can go online to www.studentscivilwar.com and learn more.

Ask your school or public librarian to help you find resources for your age!

Did you hear? There are soldiers coming to town!

I've heard rumors of war going around lately. People whispering about soldiers, weapons, strategies. Some even say I've sparked their interest. They want to fight the South and end all the slavery right now. It's the book, I guess. When I wrote Uncle Tom's Cabin, I didn't expect it to be so controversial. I just knew the story needed to be told. I wanted people to know what life was really like for slaves, with good owners and bad owners from Southern and Northern towns. I think I really got people thinking. Most have never heard slavery described like this before.—**Harriet Beecher Stowe**

I am **Tom**, a fictional character from Ms. Stowe's famous book about how slaves were mistreated. In her story, I was murdered in cold blood by plantation overseer Simon Legree. Did such things happen in real life? Were they common or rare? What do you think?

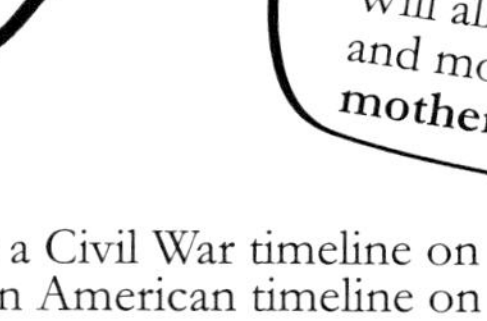

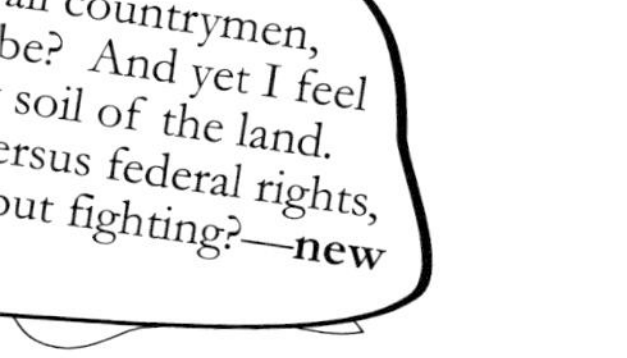

Nine months I was trying to get away.—**Solomon Northup**, slave, born free in New York, kidnapped in 1841 and enslaved on a cotton plantation near Red River in Louisiana.

I'm **Franklin Pierce**, elected president in 1852, but not strong enough to lead our nation through the gathering storm of war!

I find it so hard to believe that Americans might fight Americans! North or South, we are all countrymen, neighbors, brothers, sisters, friends—how can war be? And yet I feel this volcanic groundswell growing beneath the very soil of the land. Will all these eternal arguments over slavery, state versus federal rights, and more just grow louder until we are not talking, but fighting?—**new mother**, Georgia

 This footer is a Civil War timeline on top and an African American timeline on the bottom.

Territory, fueling debate over slave status…1808…Congress outlaws slave trade; slavery persists…1812…Louisiana joins Union as slave state…1816… Indiana

her first book of verse …1857…With the Dred Scott Decision, the U.S. Supreme Court denies citizenship to black people…1859…White abolitionist, John Brown, leads a raid at Harper's Ferry. He is captured and sentenced to death…1861…Civil

# Civil War Trivia galore...

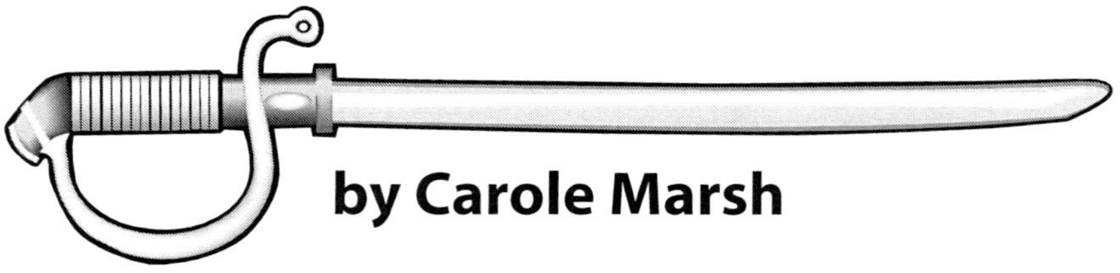

by Carole Marsh

THE BLUE AND THE GRAY
Early in the war, states, towns and wealthy individuals provided soldiers with mismatched uniforms which resulted in a confusing variety of styles and colors on the battlefield. Over time, blue became the official color for the North and gray for the South. *In the meantime, it was not uncommon for soldiers to shoot at their own men, since the uniforms were so confusing!*

GIDDY-UP!
During the Civil War, a horse was your transportation, combat vehicle, and maybe, your best friend! Robert E. Lee led the Army of Northern Virginia on his horse *Traveller*.
William Tecumseh Sherman rode *Sam* on his famous "March to the Sea."
George McClellan's horse was named *Dan Webster* after the great statesman and orator.
Ulysses S. Grant had several horses, but he was riding *Cincinnati* at the end of the war.
Stonewall Jackson was riding his favorite horse, *Little Sorrel*, when he was shot at Chancellorsville.
Jeb Stuart's famous cavalry raids were made on a horse named *Virginia*.
Union General Philip Sheridan's horse *Rienzi* is displayed at the Smithsonian Institution in Washington, D.C. *And he still looks pretty good after 150 years!*

SEARCHING FOR STONEWALL'S ARM?
After Stonewall Jackson was shot, but before he died, his arm was amputated. Jackson is buried at Lexington, Virginia in what is now known as the Stonewall Jackson Cemetery. His amputated arm was buried by the Rev. Beverly Tucker Lacy in his family burial plot about one mile from the field hospital where Jackson was initially treated. The land is now owned by the National Park Service, and there is a marker noting the location of the arm.

THE REBEL YEEEEEELLLLLLLLL!
The Rebel Yell was shouted by thousands of Confederates when they charged or were winning a fight. It's been said the bloodcurdling battle cry could provoke fear in Union troops as they faced a Confederate assault and stir the hearts of the Rebels as they summoned their courage in battle. Historians thought the sound had been lost to history until recently when it was recreated from a couple of old recordings. It is now being taught to Civil War re-enactors. Description of it is that it consisted of a high-pitched yelp, a low-pitched bark, and a long, high-pitched yelp.
*All together now:*
*YIIIIIIIII....yooooooowwwwww...YEEEEEEEEEEE EEEEEEEEEAH!*

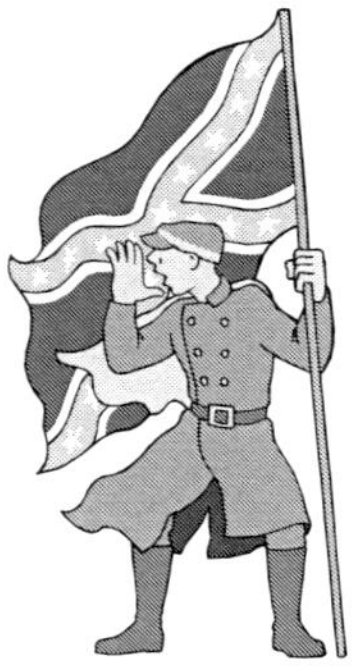

joins Union as free state...1817...Mississippi joins Union as slave state...1818...Illinois joins Union as free state...1819...Alabama joins Union as slave state...

War begins...Charlotte Forten Grimke becomes a volunteer teacher of freed men on St. Helena Island in South Carolina...1863...Harriet Tubman leads a military raid on the Combahee River in South Carolina and helps hundreds of slaves escape

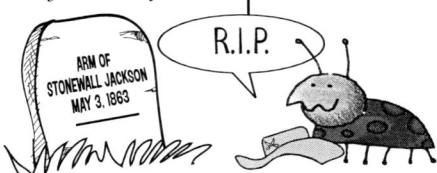

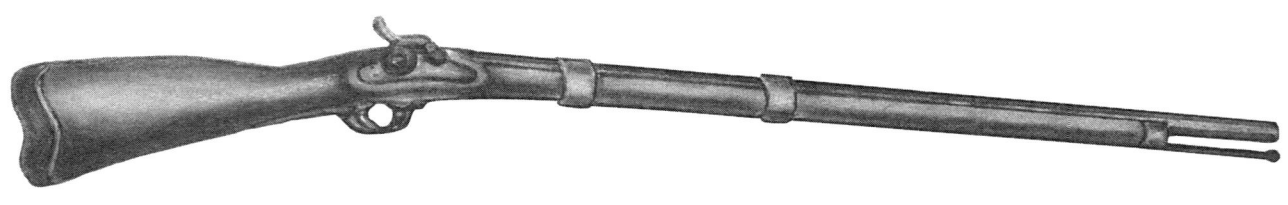

### THREE TO ONE
When the Civil War began in 1861, one out of every three people living in the South was a slave.

### BLOODY SHILOH
The battle of Shiloh in southwestern Tennessee was one of the bloodiest battles of the war. In two days, more that 23,000 men were killed, wounded, or captured. Shiloh is an ancient Hebrew word that means "place of peace." After the war, someone asked General William T. Sherman which battle was the bloodiest and most horrible. Without hesitating he said, "Shiloh."

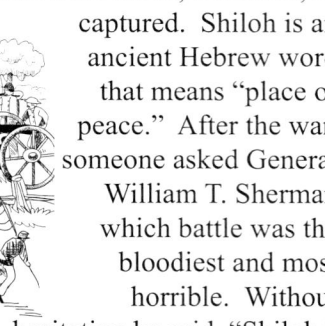

### "A RICH MAN'S WAR BUT A POOR MAN'S FIGHT"—I
A wealthy man who was drafted could hire a "substitute" to fight in his place. The Confederate Congress needed every man available so they abolished the practice in 1863, but the Union let men find a substitute if they could pay $300.

### "A RICH MAN'S WAR BUT A POOR MAN'S FIGHT"—II
Some men who did not fight made their fortunes during the war. Andrew Carnegie, J.P. Morgan, John D. Rockefeller, Charles Pillsbury, George Pullman, Jay Gould, and Marshall Field are examples. Some of these men paid a substitute $300 to take their place in the Army.

Oh, I wish I was in Dixie...

### FREE SOUTHERN SLAVES!
The Emancipation Proclamation was legally useless. It freed slaves only in the states in rebellion against the United States—where Lincoln had no authority!

### A TOUGH OL' GUY
Confederate General John Bell Hood lost the use of his left arm in battle at Gettysburg, and at Chickamauga, doctors amputated his right leg. After that, wearing a French-made cork leg, he had his aides tie him to his saddle! *Now that's gumption and never giving up!*

### MARCH TO THE SEA
On the infamous "March to the Sea," General Sherman's Army, which consisted of 60,000 battle-hardened veterans, destroyed everything in its path that could aid the Confederate war effort. They cut a path of devastation 285 miles long and 60 miles wide. *That's a lot of damage!*

### MERRY CHRISTMAS, MR. LINCOLN!
In December, 1864, General William T. Sherman sent President Lincoln a telegram that read: "I beg to present you, as a Christmas gift, the city of Savannah (Georgia), with 150 heavy guns ... and about 25,000 bales of cotton."

### EGGS FOR BREAKFAST
It's been said that General Lee had a pet chicken that traveled with him and delivered him with a fresh egg every day. *Sorry, no grits.*

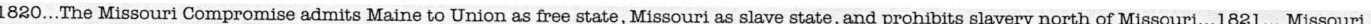

1820...The Missouri Compromise admits Maine to Union as free state, Missouri as slave state, and prohibits slavery north of Missouri...1821... Missouri

to freedom...1865...The Thirteenth Amendment abolishes slavery...The Freedmen's Bureau is established by Congress...1872...The Freedmen's Bureau is abolished by Congress...1877...The Hayes Compromise ends Reconstruction by

## WHICH STATES WERE THE "NORTH?"
California, Connecticut, Delaware, Illinois, Indiana, Iowa, Kansas, Kentucky, Maine, Maryland, Massachusetts, Michigan, Minnesota, Missouri, Nevada, New Hampshire, New Jersey, New York, Ohio, Oregon, Pennsylvania, Rhode Island, Vermont, West Virginia, and Wisconsin! The border states of Kentucky and Missouri had many people who wanted to secede but did not.

## WHICH STATES WERE THE "SOUTH?"
Seven states seceded from the United States before Abraham Lincoln took office on March 4, 1861. On December 20, 1860, South Carolina became the first state to secede. The legislature's vote was 169 for secession, 0 opposed. In less than two months, the six Deep South states seceded from the Union. Mississippi left on January 9, Florida on the 10th, Alabama on the 11th, Georgia on the 19th, Louisiana on the 26th, and Texas on February 1. After the Confederate attack on Fort Sumter on April 12, 1861, and Lincoln's call for troops on April 15, four more states declared their secession—Virginia, April 17; Arkansas, May 6; Tennessee, May 7; and North Carolina, the last state to join the Confederacy, May 20, 1861.

## TOUR A BATTLEFIELD!
If you want to take a Civil War vacation, google Civil War Tours, and you will find a bunch of battlefield tours given by professional tour guides (see civilwartours.com). There are even virtual tours that you can take on your computer! (visit nps.gov or johnsmilitaryhistory.com.) *You can visit history while wearing your pj's!*

## SLAVERY IN WASHINGTON
Slavery existed in Washington D.C., but slaves could not be brought into Washington to be bought or sold.

## WHAT IS A "CIVIL" WAR?
A civil war is a war between citizens representing different sections or groups of the same country. We still have "civil" wars around the world today. Fortunately, America has never had another civil war!

## GLORY, GLORY HALLELUJAH!
There were a lot of Civil War songs. For example, when the first Union volunteer soldiers went marching off to war, they sang a song about famed abolitionist, John Brown, who attempted to start an armed slave revolt in 1859. The song was called "John Brown's Body." Julia Ward Howe heard the song as soldiers passed in review by her window in Washington D.C. Inspired, she wrote "The Battle Hymn of the Republic," using the same tune.

## THE CLASS OF FIGHT?
Many Civil War generals on both sides knew each other since they had attended the United States Military Academy at West Point in New York. In fact, West Point's class of 1841 produced 20 Civil War generals!

## TOO GOOD TO BE TRUE?
Robert E. Lee graduated second in his class at West Point in 1829. Lee is still making history as he remains the only cadet to complete his degree without receiving a single demerit for violations of the college's very strict disciplinary code. *Go, dude! (Would we call him a nerd today?)*

## ANYONE CAN BE A GENERAL!
Confederate General George Pickett ranked last in his 1846 graduating class at West Point.

## LOST: ONE MALE SLAVE
Before the Civil War, slave traders and owners advertised in newspapers to buy and sell their slaves. "Lost and Found" sections of the paper even listed runaway slaves and offered rewards for their return.

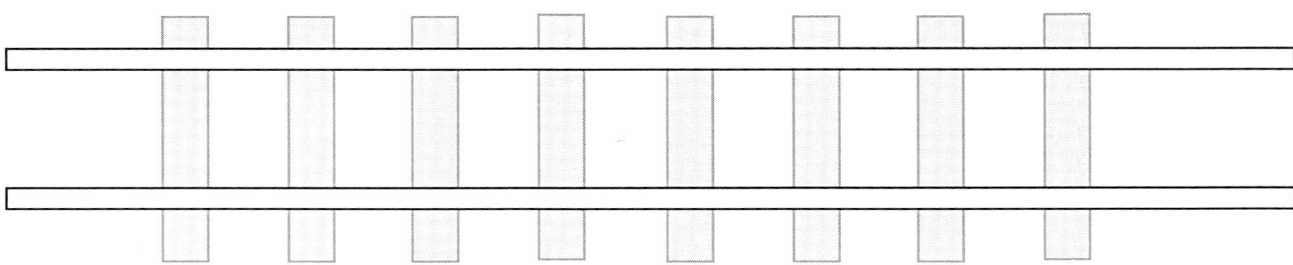

### THE GREAT (CONFUSED?) COMPROMISER
Kentucky Senator Henry Clay was called the "Great Compromiser" because he opposed a Civil War and proposed several successful compromises to postpone it. Clay had seven grandsons—three fought for the Union and four for the Confederacy. *So which side did he pull for?*

### JUST A BOY!
Edward Black, a nine-year-old musician from Indiana, was the youngest enlistee during the Civil War. He told his parents he was going to Sunday school, but instead ran off and enlisted!

### DON'T BOTHER WITH THE BANDAIDS, BROTHER!
Most Civil War rifles had bayonets on the end, but few soldiers were actually injured by these sharp swords. Single-shot muzzle loading rifles accounted for about 80% of all wounds.

### PEOPLE SPOTTING
When John Brown was hanged in Charles Town, Virginia, on December 7, 1859, there were some soon-to-be-famous faces in the crowd. Professor Thomas (Gen. Stonewall) Jackson of the Virginia Military Institute, and the 20-year-old John Wilkes Booth, a member of the Richmond militia, were watching carefully. *But what were they each thinking?*

### NORTHERN RACISM
Most abolitionists, people who wanted slavery completely abolished, lived in the North. But there was racism in the North, too. New York City mobs killed more than 100 blacks during riots there in July, 1863.

### BROTHER AGAINST BROTHER
Every Southern state except South Carolina had troops fighting for both the North and the South. *Yes, and sometimes one brother would face the other across the battle lines, and fight to the death.*

### THE FIRST ABOLITIONISTS
Quakers, who believed holding another man in servitude was a sin, were some of the first abolitionists. In 1688, a group of Quakers made the first organized protest against slavery in the American colonies. Many Quakers living in the South migrated West rather than live in a slave-based society.

### GOING UNDERGROUND
The Underground Railroad was a secret network of houses and people who illegally helped escaping slaves reach safety in the non-slave states and in Canada in the period before the Civil War. It was started by Quakers in the 1780s and was sometimes also referred to as the Liberty Line. *Like a scavenger hunt or mystery-based game, "clues" were left, such as a quilt on a fence to "point" the way the slaves should go!*

### TOOT! TOOT!
Each safe place along the Underground Railroad was called a "station," escaping slaves were called "passengers," and people who help the slaves escape were called "conductors." *A "safe" place could be a house, a basement, an attic, a barn, even squashed in a trunk!*

### DIXIE!
One of the most famous "Southern" Civil War songs was written by a Northerner. Daniel D. Emmett wrote "Dixie" in 1859 to advertise minstrel shows. The tune became an overnight sensation around the nation. Later, it became the unofficial national anthem of the Confederacy. Emmett was a native of Ohio and wrote the song in New York City! *You know it: "Oh, I wish I was in the Land of Cotton..."*

outlaws slavery...1828...South Carolina insists states can void federal laws...1830...Congress debates states' rights vs. federal government...1831...Abolitionist

Conference of Colored Women is held in Boston...1896...The U.S. Supreme Court upholds segregation in its "separate but equal" doctrine set forth in the Plessy vs. Ferguson case...Mary Church Terrell graduates from the Women's Medical

### "WHERE'S THAT STINKIN' LINCOLN?"
In the election of 1860, Abraham Lincoln did not win one Southern district and did not receive any votes in many districts because he was not even on the ballot!

### LIKE A STONE WALL
General Bernard Bee, a friend of General Stonewall Jackson's from his years at West Point, gave him his nickname on the battlefield at First Manassas on July 21, 1861. As he watched Jackson's steadfastness in the face of the enemy, Bee shouted to his troops, "Look, men, there is Jackson standing like a stone wall! Let us determine to die here, and we will conquer!"

### OLD WAR HORSE
Confederate General James Longstreet was called "Old War Horse" by General Robert E. Lee. At the Battle of the Wilderness, Longstreet was severely wounded *by his own troops. Oops!*

### 13 STARS!
Even though there were 13 stars on the Confederate battle flag, there were only 11 "Confederate states:" Virginia, Tennessee, Arkansas, Texas, Louisiana, Mississippi, Alabama, Georgia, Florida, South Carolina, and North Carolina. The other two stars were for Missouri and Kentucky. Though they technically remained in the Union, they were considered "sister states" by Confederates and furnished many thousands of Southern troops. Both elected Confederate governors and other officials. *What are friends for?!*

### LITTLE DRUMMER GIRL
Kate W. Howe enlisted in the Union army as "Tom Smith, a drummer boy." She was discovered when she was wounded at Lookout Mountain, Tennessee!

### BONNIE BLUE FLAG
"Bonnie Blue Flag" was a popular Confederate marching song that told the story of the order in which the Southern states seceded from the Union. The song was based on the flag of the same name, which was the first used by secessionists. *Later, in Margaret Mitchell's famous Civil War saga, "Gone With the Wind," Rhett Butler and Scarlett O'Hara name their daughter Bonnie Blue. She dies after a fall from her pony.*

### GREAT SCOTT!
When the state of Tennessee seceded from the Union, Scott County protested and voted to form the "Free and Independent State of Scott." *Ever had that "leave me out of it!" feeling?*

### STRIPES AND BARS? BARS AND STRIPES?
The American flag is known as the "Stars and Stripes" while the first national Confederate flag was known as the "Stars and Bars." After the first Battle of Manassas (Bull Run), the "Stars and Bars" Confederate flag was changed because it looked too much like the "Stars and Stripes" flag.

### WOMEN AT WAR!
In 1862, the *Chicago Tribune* reported that while many men were slow to respond to the war cause, both Northern and Southern women were eager to volunteer in their places. When they couldn't actually join the fighting, they volunteered as spies, mail riders, guerrillas, scouts, and saboteurs. *Some even dressed as men and served in the armies—often so successfully that when they were "found out" they were allowed to continue to serve!*

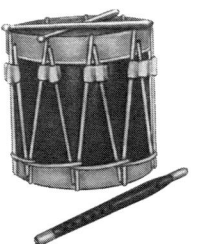

William Lloyd Garrison publishes The Liberator...Slave rebellion in Virginia leads to tougher slave laws...1832...Congress passes new tariff law, benefiting College of Pennsylvania...1909...The NAACP is founded...1920...The Nineteenth Amendment gives women the right to vote...1935...Federal Writers' Project established by Franklin Roosevelt...fieldworkers were assigned to travel through

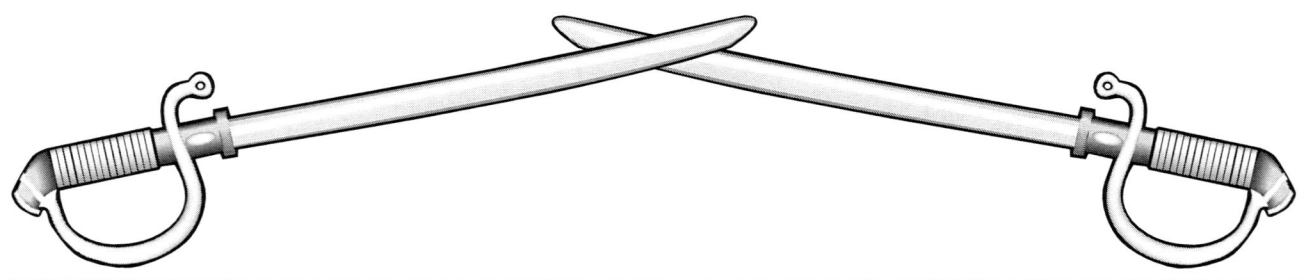

### THE NANCY HARTS
The women in Troup County, Georgia, formed a home guard called the "Nancy Harts" in honor of a Georgian heroine of the American Revolution. The Nancy Harts had rifles and muskets and made their own ammunition!

### HARRIET TUBMAN
Escaping from slavery in 1849, Harriet Tubman assisted the Union Army as a cook, nurse, armed scout, and spy during the Civil War. She was the first woman to lead an armed expedition in the war when she guided a raid that liberated more than 700 slaves!

### A WOMAN AT BULL RUN
Augusta Foster from Maine fought at the Battle of Bull Run. She had her horse shot from under her but was able to escape to Alexandria. *You could say she was "on the run!"*

### A WOMAN AT ANTIETAM
Mary Galloway fought at Antietam. She enlisted to be near her husband. Mary was wounded, and Clara Barton cared for her during her recovery. The Galloways later named their child after Clara!

### A WOMAN'S DUTY
Katie Beattie was a spy, smuggler, and saboteur who torched warehouses and Federal boats and successfully helped many prisoners escape—all for the Southern cause.

### THE GARDENER TOLD ALL!
John Watt, President Lincoln's gardener at the White House, confessed to selling official secrets to a newspaper. He was trusted by the President's family because he was a favorite of Mary Todd Lincoln. *And I thought it was always the butler who did it!*

### BELLE OF VIRGINIA
In early 1862, 18-year-old Belle Boyd was the Southern belle of Fort Royal, Virginia. She used her charm to spy for the South. Once, she raced her horse, Fleeta, 54 miles over mountainous terrain to deliver a packet of Federal papers to General Stonewall Jackson. Captured by Yankees, she was later released and fled to London in 1863, where she became a stage actress. *After all, she'd had a lot of practice!*

### CIVIL WAR POPULATION
At the start of the war, the population of the North was about 22 million people. The South had about 9 million, 3.5 million of whom were slaves.

### CONFEDERATE CAPITALS
Montgomery, Alabama was the first capital of the Confederacy and the site of Mississippian Jefferson Davis' presidential inauguration. The capital was later moved to Richmond, Virginia to be closer to the war. *Yeah, that's always my plan—get in the line of fire?!*

### UNION GENERAL LEE?!
At the beginning of the war, Robert E. Lee was asked to command the Union's Federal Army, but he rejected the offer because he knew the job would eventually include an invasion of his beloved state of Virginia. Instead, he accepted the command of the Confederate's Virginia State Militia. *And I guess you call that a real "About face!"*

### THOSE NEW ORLEANS WOMEN!
The women of New Orleans took special pleasure in offending Federal occupation troops. They wore Confederate insignia on their dresses and held their noses when Yankees passed by*! Today, we just say "Nanny, nanny, boo, boo!"*

Northern industry...South Carolina nullifies federal edict, calls for secession...President Jackson declares no states may leave Union...1833...Lucretia Mott

Southern states to gather life histories of ex-slaves...1940...Ella Jo Baker, a dedicated organizer in the freedom movement, begins work in the South as field secretary of the NAACP...1941...Civil Rights Movement begins...Thousands of black

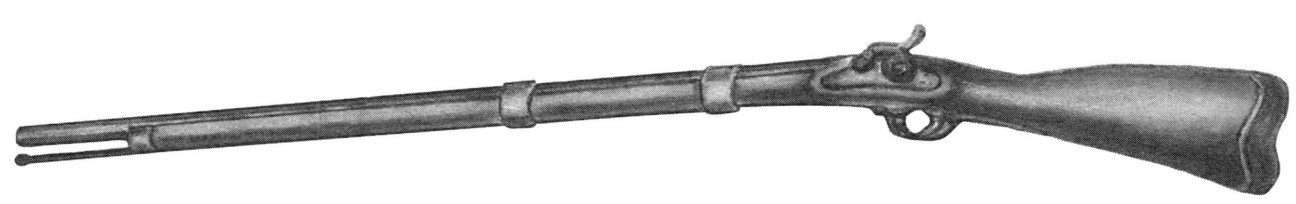

CALL IT WHAT YOU WILL!
The American Civil War is know by many different names, some of them being: The War Between the States, Mr. Lincoln's War, the Second American Revolution, The Great Rebellion, the War for the Union, the Brothers' War, the War to Suppress Yankee Arrogance, the Yankee Invasion, the Lost Cause, and the War of Northern Aggression. *Among, oh, about 100 more!*

WHOSE SIDE ARE YOU ON, ANYWAY?
Abraham Lincoln had four brothers-in-law—all of whom fought for the Confederacy! *Relatives! Whatcha gonna do with 'em?!*

FIRE IN THE HOLE!
The first shots of the Civil War took place at Fort Sumter in Charleston Harbor, South Carolina. For 48 straight hours, Confederate artillery battered the fort, firing more than 3,000 shells. Not a single man on either side was killed during the bombardment. *Well, see, we were just getting' warmed up, ya'll.*

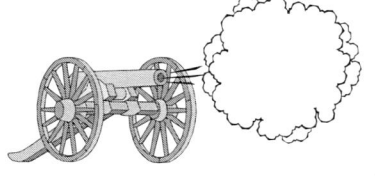

SOS!
The fastest way to send a message during the Civil War was by telegraph. Before the telegraph, messages could be sent only by horseback or sailing ship. With the telegraph, a message could be sent almost as fast as the telegrapher could tap the keys. Using Morse Code, a code invented by Samuel Morse who also invented the telegraph, an operator tapped out the dot-and-dash message. The short and long taps were carried over the telegraph wires as short and long electrical impulses to the receiving end, where another telegrapher wrote out the message. By the early 1860s, telegraph wires connected all the cities and towns east of the Mississippi River, and lines were stretching westward. A message could be transmitted hundreds of miles in a matter of seconds. Ships at sea used lanterns to flash messages in the same code.

LITTLE TIN SOLDIERS
During the Civil War years, children played with hand-carved wooden toys and manufactured toys made from thin pieces of tin. The tin toys were very popular because the toy companies could add little windup springs that made the toys move. But the tin was so flimsy that the toys quickly fell apart or broke. Gradually, in the 1860s, toy manufacturers turned to iron, which was solid but too heavy for a windup mechanism. Instead, toymakers built them with wheels so children could pull them. From then through the early 1900s, millions of iron toys were made. Circus wagons, fire engines, and railroad steam engines were very popular. *And valuable collector's items today, if you can find them! Check grandma's attic!*

AFRICAN AMERICAN SOLDIERS
An estimated 186,000 African Americans served in the Union Army, and another 30,000 in the Navy. These volunteers were segregated, or separated, in "colored regiments," with white officers over them. African American soldiers took part in 39 major battles with 16 men receiving the Congressional Medal of Honor, the highest award for bravery!

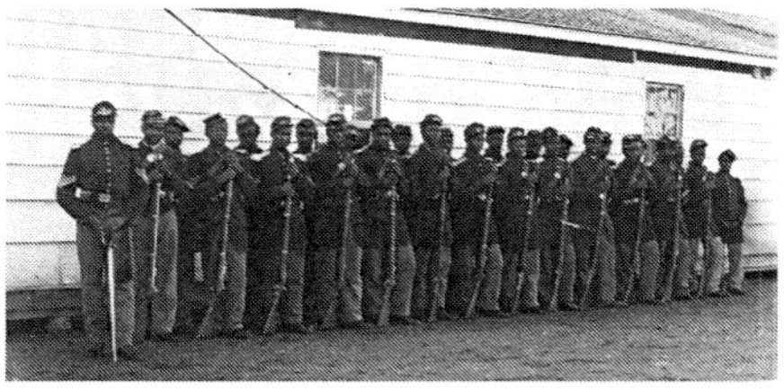

CIVIL WAR SOCIALIZING
At the end of a battle day, soldiers stood guard in advance of their army camp for the night. Often, these guards, called pickets, were within feet of pickets of the opposing army. The men would exchange jokes, Northern coffee for Southern tobacco, and opinions of the day's battle. Out of respect for the unprotected position of these soldiers, there was no firing by either side at these men on picket duty.

forms Female Anti-Slavery Society...Theodore Weld forms American Anti-Slavery Society...Ohio's Oberlin College 1st to admit blacks...1835... South Carolina

*people organize to press their demands for justice... President Roosevelt issues an executive order against discrimination of workers in defense industries and government...1942... Margaret Walker wins the Yale Award for Young Poets for her*

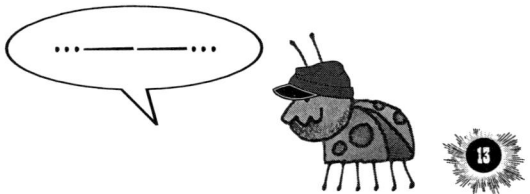

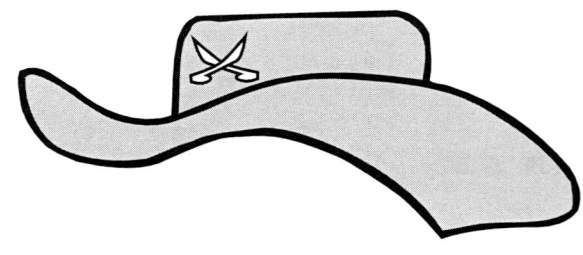

### SCHOOL BELLS!
By 1860, most cities in the North offered free public elementary schools. Public schools in the South and in frontier areas were few in number and far apart. Public high schools developed even more slowly. When the Civil War began in 1861, there were fewer than 70 public high schools in the entire country. There were more than 6,000 private schools, however, where parents paid a tuition fee to send their children. *But did they have tests?!*

### AFRICAN AMERICAN SCHOOLS
African American children had very limited opportunities for education. In fact, in the South it was against the law to teach slaves to read and write. Some free African Americans, however, in both the North and the South, did manage to go to school, usually at private institutions operated by religious groups.

### THE COTTON GIN
In 1793, Eli Whitney invented a simple, hand-cranked machine called a cotton gin. The gin separated the cotton fibers from its sticky seeds 50 times faster than could be done by hand. It made growing cotton much more economical for cotton farmers and plantation owners. At the same time, other inventions made it possible for mills in New England and in England to produce huge quantities of cotton fabric. The mills could use all the cotton the South could produce! *Loopholes in the patent laws back then left Whitney with little profits for his cotton gin – instead he became rich by figuring out how to mass produce muskets!*

### KING COTTON!
After the invention of the cotton gin, cotton became the South's most important product. It was such a valuable cash crop—a crop that could be sold for profit—that people called it "King Cotton." *Until the evil "boll weevil" came along!*

### EQUAL TIME!
At Fredericksburg, Virginia, during the war's second winter, a crack group of Union musicians making camp on the northern bank of the Rapahannock River staged a unique concert. The program began with a medley of Northern patriotic tunes and war songs. "Now, give us one of ours!" shouted the Confederates camped across the river. The band immediately struck up "Dixie," "My Maryland," and "The Bonnie Blue Flag"—all tunes of the South!

### CIVIL WAR MUSIC
Some songs written during the Civil War days include "Tenting Tonight," "Tramp, Tramp, Tramp," "Dixie," "Aura Lea," "Love Me Tender," "The Yellow Rose of Texas," and the "Battle Hymn of the Republic." *Sing it again, Elvis!*

### SHIPS AHOY!
When the war began, the Union Navy had 42 ships on active duty. By war's end, that number had increased to nearly 700!

### CONFEDERATE NAVY
There was no Confederate Navy when the Civil War began. The Confederacy purchased a total of 18 ships built in England and had them outfitted for war…in other countries!

burns abolitionist literature…Georgia threatens to enact death penalty for abolitionist writers…Abolitionist William Ellery Channing publishes Slavery…1836

moving collection of poems, "For My People"…1947…Lawyer and economist, Sadie T.M. Alexander is appointed to Truman's Commission on Civil Rights…CORE sends its first group of "Freedom Riders" through the South…1948…President

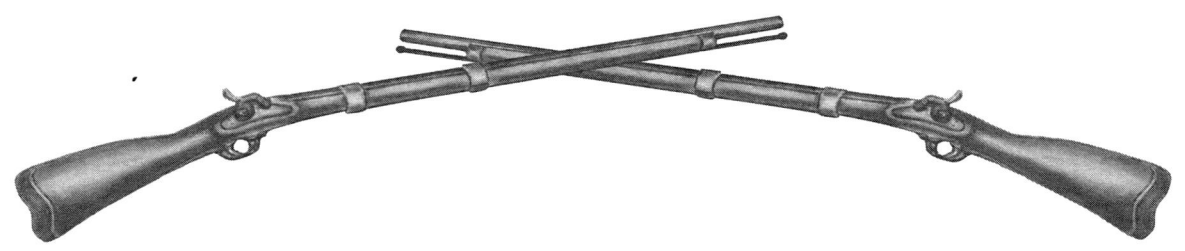

### ANOTHER ONE SUNK, AND ANOTHER, AND ANOTHER…
The *Alabama* and the *Florida* were two of the most infamous Confederate raiding ships. Between them, they sank a total of 102 Union ships!

### OH, SHENANDOAH!
The Confederate ship *Shenandoah* sank 38 Union ships and her crew captured more than 1,000 Union seamen and did more than 1 million dollars in damage to the Northern cause. She continued to fight three months after General Lee surrendered and made her last capture off the coast of Alaska!
*And then did she head to Siberia?!*

### COLOR-CODED
For both the Union and Confederate armies: red trim and striping on the trousers of a soldier's uniform meant he was in the artillery, blue meant he was in the infantry, and yellow meant he was in the cavalry.

### HEY, YOU BUTTERNUTS!
Because of shortages of material, many Southern soldiers dyed their own clothes at home before enlisting. The dye turned their clothes a dull yellow-brown. In time, Southern soldiers became known as "Butternuts."

### BILLY AND JOHNNY
Union soldiers called Confederate soldiers "Johnny Reb." Johnny Rebs called Union soldiers "Billy Yank."

### MEANT FOR WAR?
The Battle of Manassas, or Bull Run, took place near the home of Wilmer McLean. During the fighting, a cannonball crashed through his house, causing great damage to the structure and distress to his wife and children. When McLean relocated his family to a small village called Appomattox Court House, about 20 miles east of Lynchburg, he assumed they had escaped the dangerous sights and sounds of the war's front lines for good. However, in a strange coincidence, the war entered the lives of the McLean family again when they witnessed its conclusion at close range. Generals Lee and Grant used the front parlor of the McLean's second home to sign the terms of surrender for the Army of Northern Virginia!

### BUT WHERE DID IT HAPPEN?
Civil War battle names varied depending on who was talking about it—a Northerner or a Southerner. Federals often named battles after nearby streams or rivers, while Confederates named them for nearby towns or communities. For example:

| Federal | Confederate |
| --- | --- |
| Bull Run | Manassas Junction |
| Antietam Creek | Sharpsburg |
| Stone's River | Murfreesboro |
| Pittsburg Landing | Shiloh |

### HE'S MY ROOMMATE!
Simon Bolivar Buckner was Ulysses S. Grant's roommate at West Point, and later surrendered to him at Fort Donelson, Tennessee, in 1862.

### THE GRAY GHOST
Confederate cavalry commander John Singleton Mosby was famous for his lightning quick raids and his ability to elude the Union Army. He and his men would escape by blending in with local farmers and townspeople, particularly those in eastern Virginia where he was very popular. His battalion was known as Mosby's Raiders, and Mosby was given the nickname the "Gray Ghost."

…Arkansas joins Union as slave state…1837…Michigan joins Union as free state…1845…Florida joins Union as slave state…Texas joins union as slave state

Truman issues an executive order banning segregation in the armed forces…Pharmacist Ella Nora Phillips Stewart is elected president of the National Association of Colored Women…Edith Irby Jones is the first black to be admitted to a Southern

### BATTLE OF THE IRONCLADS
The Civil War battle of the Ironclads, between the Union *Monitor* and Confederate *Virginia* (or *Merrimac*) was fought in the Hampton Roads Harbor on March 8 - 9, 1862. The outcome was a draw. But the battle marked the end of wooden Navy boats! The *Monitor* sank in a gale off Cape Hatteras, North Carolina in late 1862.

### THE CONFEDERACY WANTS YOU!
The Confederate government established a military draft on April 16, 1862. It called for all males ages 18-35 to be inducted into the Army for three years. By February 1864, the draft was expanded to include all males from 17-50.

### IT'S MINE! NO, IT'S MINE!
The Shenandoah Valley was the most fought after area in the nation during the Civil War. The town of Winchester, Virginia, changed hands 76 times! *Residents must have stayed confused?*

### IT'S TOO COLD!
For the most part, military campaigns in the war started in the spring and continued until cold weather set in. There was very little fighting in the winter months. An exception is the Battle of Stones River in Murfreesboro, Tennessee, on December 30-31, 1862, one of the war's bloodiest but with no clear winner! It was fought in rain, sleet, and fog, and had so many dead bodies littering the battlefield that it was referred to as the "slaughter pen."

### BRING IN THE IRISH!
More than 160,000 Irish-born men fought for the Union, most serving in all-Irish units. Brigadier General Thomas Meagher and his "Irish Brigade" fought in the legendary battles at Antietam and Fredericksburg. *But did they have the "luck" of the Irish?*

### NOW THAT'S A TRENCH!
In 1862 at Fredericksburg, Virginia, Confederate trenches stretched for 7 miles!

### MEDICINE SMUGGLING
In the South, medicines were expensive and hard to come by. Doctors and nurses turned to herbs, but they desperately needed quinine, morphine, and chloroform for painkillers. To get them, they had to be smuggled out of the North. Most of this smuggling was done by women who hid the medicine in their clothes, petticoats, parasols, and suitcases with false bottoms!

### PRESIDENT UNDER FIRE!
President Lincoln is the only American president ever exposed to enemy fire while in office—once on board a tugboat in 1862 and once during a raid on Washington, D.C.'s outer defenses in 1864! *No Secret Service back then!*

### EXTRA! EXTRA!
Newspapers in both the North and the South were officially censored during the Civil War. No military news could be printed without approval of the general officer in command.

### THE PRICE OF GOLD
As the war progressed and their gold supply vanished, the value of Confederate money declined. In 1862, $120 bought $100 in gold. By the end of the war, $5,500 bought $100 in gold. *But today, it's a collector's item!*

### GLORY!
The 54th Massachusetts Regiment, led by Colonel Robert Gould Shaw, was the first African American regiment. The story of the regiment was told in the 1990 film, *Glory*.

### CHARGE!
The Battle of Brandy Station in Virginia on June 9, 1863, was the largest cavalry battle ever to take place in the Western Hemisphere—19,000 men and their horses fought in the 12-hour battle.

### LET US BACK IN!
On June 20, 1863, Virginia's northernmost counties seceded back into the Union and formed the new state of West Virginia.

### GREAT GOBS OF GETTYSBURG!
The Battle of Gettysburg in Pennsylvania was the largest land battle ever fought in the Western Hemisphere. In just three days of fighting, more than 50,000 Federal and Confederate soldiers were killed, wounded, or captured!

•More than 3,000 horses were killed. The 9th Massachusetts Artillery Battalion lost 80 of its 88 horses.

•The 26th North Carolina Infantry went into the Battle of Gettysburg with 800 men. By the end of the battle, only 86 survived.

•17 of the 51 Confederate generals who rode to Gettysburg with General Lee died during the battle.

### HOLD LITTLE ROUND TOP!
With about 200 men, the 20th Maine Infantry under the command of Joshua Lawrence Chamberlain defended a small rocky hill called Little Round Top fending off several brigades of Confederate infantry for several hours at Gettysburg. Chamberlain received the Congressional Medal of Honor for bravery and service to his country.

•Major General Daniel Sickles lost his leg during the Battle of Round Top. Later, he donated the amputated limb to a medical museum and was known to visit it frequently after the war!

•The massive military barrage of cannon that occurred right before General Pickett's Charge at Gettysburg could be heard 140 miles away in Pittsburg!

•At Gettysburg, General Pickett commanded the famous charge that bears his name—Pickett's Charge. During the assault, all 3 brigadier generals and 13 colonels who took part were either killed or badly wounded. Pickett's division lost over two-thirds of its men.

•Confederate troops from North Carolina advanced farthest in Pickett's Charge at Gettysburg and were some of the last troops to surrender at Appomattox.

•After the Battle of Gettysburg, the Federal Army's Ordinance Bureau recovered nearly 30,000 rifles and muskets.

•Gettysburg has been called the "high water mark" of the Confederacy because after losing that battle, the Army of Northern Virginia never launched a major offensive again and was slowly worn down by superior Union numbers and resources.

### VERY VICKSBURG!

### UNDER SIEGE? NO, UNDER HORSE!
During the Vicksburg campaign, General Ulysses S. Grant was injured when his horse slipped on a muddy river bank and fell on him!

### I PROMISE NOT TO RE-ENLIST!
After the siege of Vicksburg, General Grant held 30,000 Confederate prisoners. Instead of shipping them north as POWs (Prisoners of War), he paroled the soldiers. They pledged to not re-enlist and take up arms again for the Confederacy.

### RIDE ON!
Wounded in action several times, General Nathan Bedford Forrest had 29 horses shot out from under him in battle!

*Hey, I'm a little round top!*

1850...Congress passes the Compromise of 1850...1852...Harriet Beecher Stowe publishes Uncle Tom's Cabin...1854...Congress passes the Kansas-Nebraska
deliberate speed."...In Montgomery, Alabama, Rosa Parks refuses to give up her seat on a public bus to a white man. She is arrested and jailed...A year-long bus boycott results in the U.S. Supreme Court invalidating segregation on Montgomery

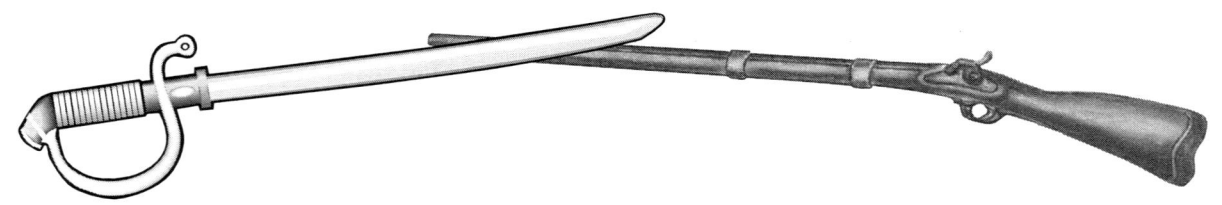

### THE FIRST SUBMARINE
The Confederacy sent the world's first successful submarine, the *H. L. Hunley*, into action in Charleston Harbor on February 17, 1864. The sub sank the Union's *USS Housatonic*; but soon after the *Hunley* also sank, drowning all eight crewmen. On August 8, 2000, the wreck was finally recovered and the DNA-identified remains of the eight *Hunley* crew members were interred in Charleston's Magnolia Cemetery with full military honors several years later.

### LEE'S HOME
Unable to pay their property taxes in person—as required by law—General Lee and his wife, Mary Custis Lee, lost Arlington House (her estate) when the Federal government confiscated it in 1864. In order to prevent the Lees from recovering the property, part of the property became the nucleus of Arlington National Cemetery

### THE WILDERNESS
Between May 5 and June 30, 1864, as General Grant pushed toward Richmond, the Army of the Potomac suffered more than 61,000 casualties. In one 20-minute stretch of battle at a location called Cold Harbor, 7,000 Union soldiers fell during an assault against Rebels who were fortified in trenches. All total, General Grant's losses exceeded the total strength of Lee's Army at any one time!

### STRANGE CIRCUMSTANCES
One year after Stonewall Jackson was shot at the Battle of Chancellorsville, Confederate General James Longstreet was wounded less than three miles from the spot where Jackson fell. In both cases, the generals were accidentally shot by their own troops. Unlike Jackson, Longstreet survived the wound and served with Lee until the end of the war.

### THE LONGEST SIEGE
When Ulysses S. Grant failed to capture Richmond in the spring of 1864, he attempted to cut off General Lee's supply line by laying siege to Petersburg a few miles away. The siege lasted for 9 and 1/2 months, making it the longest siege in United States history!

### THE FIELD OF MUDDY SHOES
Virginia Military Institute cadets, some as young as 14 years old, fought in the Battle of New Market in Virginia in May 1864. The cadets charged across a muddy field—later named the "Field of Lost Shoes"—and helped to break the Union lines.

### JEFFERSON DAVIS
After the Civil War, Confederate President Jefferson Davis was imprisoned in Fort Monroe for two years. He lost his U.S. citizenship and died a man without a country. One hundred years later, President Jimmy Carter restored Davis's citizenship. Today, the fort's Casemate Museum has preserved the cell Davis once occupied. *Who was the other famous "Man Without a Country" in U.S. history?*

### SURPRISING SLAVE NUMBERS
At the beginning of the Civil War, only about 10,000 families owned more than 50 slaves; three-quarters of all Southern families owned no slaves.

### IS IT OVER YET?
Word was slow to travel in Civil War days. The last skirmish occurred after the war officially ended. It happened on May 13, 1865, near Brownsville, Texas. Ironically, the Union troops retreated, giving the Confederates a victory. Several days later, on May 26, the Confederate troops got word of the war's end and surrendered.

Act...1856...Proslavery candidate James Buchanan elected president...1857...Supreme Court rules escaped slave Dred Scott is property that must be returned

buses...1957...As president of the state NAACP, Daisy Gatson Bates leads the fight for school integration in Little Rock, Arkansas...1960...First student sit-ins at a lunch counter in Greensboro, North Carolina...1961...More than 50,000 people

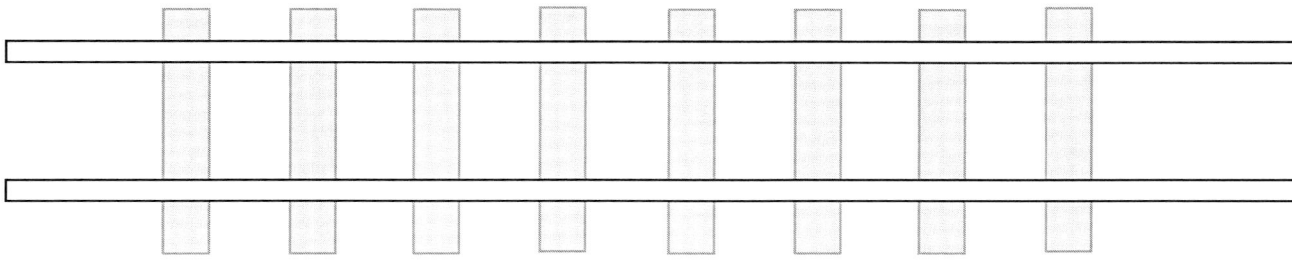

### UNION TROOPS
When the Civil War began, the United States had 15,259 enlisted men and 1,108 officers on active duty. By the war's end, nearly 3 million men served in the military.

### A MODERN WAR
Called the first "modern war," the Civil War introduce many "firsts": the U. S. Secret Service; the Medal of Honor; the income tax; a viable machine gun; naval torpedoes; repeating rifles; battlefield photography; and the first African American Army officer, Major M. R. Delany.

### LET'S ROLL!
The Civil War had nearly 6,000 skirmishes and battles.

### THAT'S A LOT OF HORSES!
By the time General Lee surrendered, the U. S. government had bought and paid for about 840,000 horses and 430,000 mules.

### POWs
Prisoners-of-war suffered in prisons in both the South and the North. Exposure to inclement weather, disease, hunger, tainted drinking water, and foul sanitary conditions took a horrible death toll. Of nearly 200,000 prisoners held in the South, about 30,000 died. In the North, nearly the same number died of the 230,000 prisoners held.

### NATIVE AMERICAN SOLDIERS
Of the 3,530 Native Americans who fought in the Union Army, 1,018, or nearly one-third, died.

### AFRICAN AMERICAN DEATHS
About 180,000 African Americans fought for the North and more than 36,000 gave their lives.

### AFRICAN AMERICAN SOLDIERS
An unknown number of African Americans served in the Confederate Army, including 45 men with General Nathan Bedford Forrest. Of those, 44 survived the war, and 38 went with him to work in his farming operation in Mississippi after the war.

### WAR CRIMES
The only man arrested and convicted of war crimes during the Civil War was Henry Wirz, the commandant of the notorious Andersonville Prison in Georgia. The U.S. government arrested, tried, convicted, and hanged him for starving the disease-ridden Union prisoners under his command.

### ANDERSONVILLE VS. ELMIRA
The percentage of deaths at the Confederate Prison of Andersonville in Georgia was only slightly higher than at the Union prison camp at Elmira, New York.

### LIFE AFTER WAR
After the war, a number of generals achieved success:
- Robert E. Lee became president of Washington College in Lexington, Virginia. Today the college is named Washington and Lee University.
- In 1869, William T. Sherman became the highest-ranking general in the U.S. Army.
- James Longstreet held many federal positions, including surveyor of customs in New Orleans, minister to Turkey, and U.S. marshal for Georgia.
- Residents of Maine elected Joshua L. Chamberlain, who held Little Round Top at Gettysburg, governor four consecutive times.
- Six Union officers became U.S. Presidents: Ulysses S. Grant, Chester A. Arthur, James A. Garfield, Benjamin Harrison, Rutherford B. Hayes, and William McKinley.

### STRIKE THE TENT!
In 1870, Robert E. Lee fell ill at his home in Lexington, Virginia, and died in his parlor. It is said his last words were, "Strike the tent."

### LAST CIVIL WAR VETERAN
Walter Williams, the last reported surviving Civil War veteran, died on December 19, 1959, at the age of 117. Once a forager for Confederate General John Bell Hood, Williams survived the last of the Union veterans by three years. *Wouldn't it have been fascinating to talk to him?!*

### CAREFUL WHERE YOU SIT!
A Civil War soldier usually carried a blanket bedroll with extra clothing, personal items, and a poncho (waterproof covering). He also carried a cartridge box with about 40 rounds of ammunition. If there was time before a battle, soldiers were issued extra ammo, which they usually carried in their pockets.

### DOG TENTS
Every Union soldier was issued a small, two-man tent that was one rectangular piece of canvas buttoned to another. The tent could be pitched by tying each end to a rifle stuck in the ground by its bayonet. The men called the tents "dog tents" because they joked that only a dog could crawl under it and stay dry from the rain. Confederate soldiers did not receive shelter tents, but as the war progressed, it was common to see captured Union tents in a Rebel camp!

### THE DRUM
For the infantry, drums were used to announce daily activities, from sunrise to sunset. Reveille was sounded to begin the day at 5 a.m. Drummers were also important on the march to keep soldiers in step during parades and to call them to attention. In battle, drums were sometimes used to signal maneuvers and give signals for the ranks to load and fire their weapons. *Pa-rum-pa-pa-pum was pretty important!*

### THE BUGLE
The artillery and cavalry relied solely on buglers who were as important in their roles as the drummers were to the infantry.

### THE BAND
When not playing for their respective regiments, musicians were often combined with regimental or brigade bands to play marching tunes or provide field music for parades, inspections, and reviews.

### UNION CAMP FOOD
Union soldiers usually had enough to eat when an army was in camp, but the meals were pretty boring—dried beef or bacon, beans or peas, bread, and coffee. Officers enjoyed the best food, and some even brought their own cooks and personal servants. The rations were even more tiresome when the army was on the move. Each soldier carried hardtack, salt pork, coffee, and a little sugar and salt. To improve their diet, the men foraged, or lived off the land. They bought—or simply took—whatever crops and farm animals they could find. *And the hardtack was often riddled with weevils!*

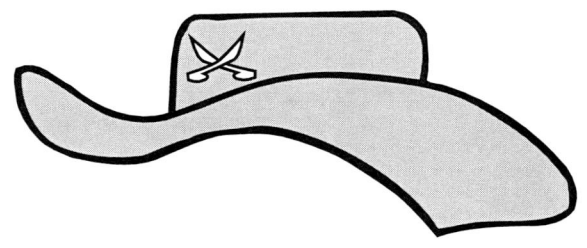

### SUTLERS
Food suppliers, called sutlers, set up tents in the camps where they sold eggs, coffee, fresh meat, newspapers, shoelaces, cigars, candy, and other hard-to-get items—usually at exorbitant prices—to the soldiers, who were eager for such rare wartime treats.

### SOUTHERN CAMP FOOD
Southern soldiers usually had a lot less to eat than Union soldiers. Bacon, cornmeal, molasses, peas, tobacco, vegetables, and rice were part of their diet. They usually did not have real coffee unless they were able to trade some tobacco for coffee with a Union soldier.

### YUCK!
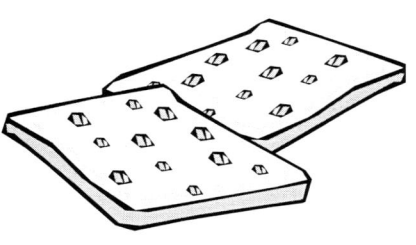
Hardtack, a dry flour cracker so hard that it often had to be broken with a rifle butt, was a basic part of a soldier's diet. *And don't forget those weevils!*

### WELL WORTH THE MONEY
In 1863, a private in the Union Army received $13.00 a month.

### A SOLDIER AND HIS PET
Although it was against regulations, soldiers often had pets, including cats, squirrels, raccoons, and especially dogs. The 11th Pennsylvania had an unofficial mascot named Sallie, who followed them into combat. There is a bronze statue of Sallie on the regimental monument at Gettysburg.
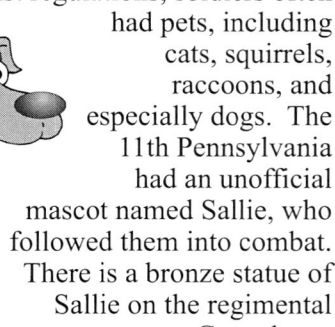

### ARMS AND THE INFANTRYMAN
Usually, an infantryman carried a muzzle-loading rifle-musket manufactured in American arsenals or one purchased from foreign countries, such as England. A steel bayonet was positioned on the muzzle and was very imposing although most soldiers did not use the bayonet much in battle. When not in battle, the bayonet was a handy candle holder and useful in grinding coffee beans. The typical rifle-musket weighed 8.5 pounds and fired a conical shaped bullet called the Minie Ball. Bullets were made of very soft lead and caused horrible wounds which were difficult to heal.

### THE ARTILLERY
Artillery are the large-caliber guns used in warfare. The Civil War artillery was composed of both rifled and smoothbore cannon. A crew of 14 men, including the drivers, served each gun. The role of the artillery was to support the infantry, while the infantry role was to either attack or defend, depending on the circumstances. Both branches worked together to coordinate their tactics on the field of battle.

### SEND IN THE CAVALRY!
Cavalrymen were armed with breech loading carbines, sabers, and pistols. Initially, cavalry troops were used for scouting purposes and to guard supply trains. By the Battle of Gettysburg, though, the role of mounted troops expanded, with cavalry divisions acting as skirmishers and fighting mounted and on foot in pitched battles (a planned military encounter on a prearranged battleground), such as Brandy Station. *And they weren't just horsin' around!*

Abraham Lincoln elected president...South Carolina votes to secede from the Union...1861...Florida, Alabama, Georgia, Mississippi, and Louisiana secede from

facilities; in employment on the basis of sex, religion, nationality; and establishes the Equal Employment Opportunity Commission... Lawyer, Marion Wright Edelman establishes the NAACP's Legal Defense and Education Fund Office in Jackson,

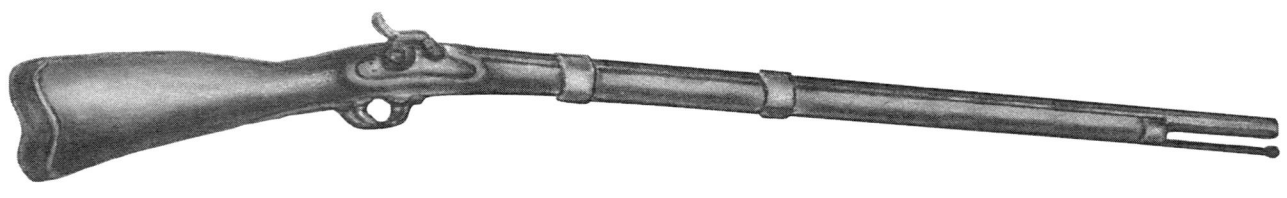

### ROUNDING OUT THE ARMY
Besides the infantry, artillery, and cavalry, other branches of the armies included the signal corps, engineers, medical and hospital corps, and supply organizations, including the quartermasters. *It takes a "village" to go to war!*

### FIRST SHOT MISSED!
The first shot of the Battle of Gettysburg was fired by an Illinois cavalry officer who used a carbine borrowed from his sergeant. The officer missed his target. *No auspicious start, hey?*

### GETTYSBURG MEMORIAL
Veterans of the North and the South worked together to build the Eternal Light Peace Memorial at Gettysburg National Military Park. President Franklin D. Roosevelt dedicated it on July 3, 1938, during the 75th Anniversary celebration of the battle of Gettysburg. *Peace, at last!*

### HIGH WATER MARK
The High Water Mark Monument at Gettysburg National Military Park lists the commands of both armies that participated in "Pickett's Charge," the last great Southern attack at Gettysburg. "High Water Mark" refers to a location on Cemetery Ridge where Pickett's men were able to breach a place called "the Angle," but the Union line was quickly closed and any Rebels were killed or captured. This was considered the Confederacy's last best chance of winning the war.

### REUNION!
In July 1913, more than 50,000 Union and Confederate veterans held a reunion at Gettysburg National Military Park to celebrate the 50th anniversary of the battle. *And a good time was had by all, unlike 50 years earlier!*

### ON THE JOB TRAINING?
Major General George Gordon Meade, commander of the Union Army of the Potomac at the Battle of Gettysburg, was assigned to command the army just three days before the battle. *And yet, he rose to the occasion!*

### THE WIDOW'S HOME
The simple farmhouse home of widow Lydia Lester was used as a headquarters by Union General George G. Meade during the Battle of Gettysburg in 1863. The house still stands today and can be seen on a visit to Gettysburg National Military Park. *And if those walls could talk!*

### WHAT'S IN A NAME?
Union forces mostly named their armies after rivers, while Confederates named their armies after geographical locations. For example, the Army of Tennessee was a Confederate Army. The Army of the Tennessee (River) was a Union Army.

### SHILOH
The Battle of Shiloh in Tennessee took its name from a small log church that sat on the battlefield. The original Shiloh Church survived the battle but was destroyed in the weeks after the fight.

### KILLED IN ACTION
The Confederate Army commander, General Albert Sidney Johnston, was killed at Shiloh on April 6, 1862. In all of American history, he is the highest-ranking American military officer ever to be killed in action.

### MIDNIGHT TRAIN TO MANASSAS
During the First Manassas campaign, Confederate reinforcements traveled by train to the frontlines of the battle. The 35-mile trip was the first time in American history that railroads were tactically used to move soldiers to a battle.

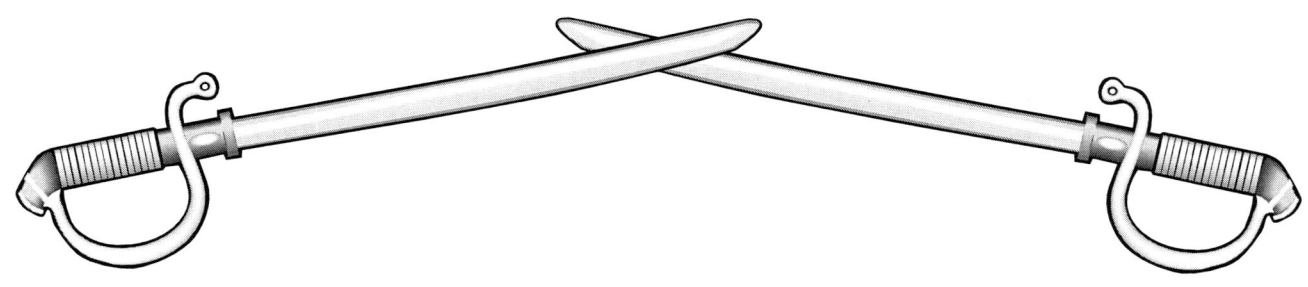

### SEMPER FI
While commanding a Union battery at First Manassas, Captain James Ricketts was wounded and captured. His wife Fannie found him at a field hospital and went with her husband to a Richmond prison to nurse him back to health. Ricketts survived and ended the war a Major General.

### JUDITH HENRY
Only one civilian was killed during the battle of Bull Run. Judith Carter Henry, an 85-year-old bedridden widow, was mortally wounded by Union artillery fire.

### PHOTOS OF ANTIETAM
Alexander Gardner's photographs of the Battle of Antietam were the first ever images to show dead soldiers on the field of battle. A *New York Times* article about the photographs said it was as if the "dead had been laid at our doorsteps."

### BRAVE BUGLE BOY

Private Johnny Cook, a bugler with Battery B, 4th U.S., was awarded the Medal of Honor for his actions at Antietam when he was only 15 years old!

### CAPTAIN SHAW AT ANTIETAM
Robert Gould Shaw served as a Captain in the 2nd Massachusetts Infantry and was wounded in the Cornfield at Antietam before taking command of the 54th Massachusetts Infantry made famous in the movie *Glory*.

### 1ST TEXAS INFANTRY
The First Texas Infantry lost 82% of their men killed, wounded and missing while fighting in the Cornfield at Antietam, the highest casualty rate for any Confederate regiment in one battle of the Civil War!

### LINCOLN AT ANTIETAM
President Abraham Lincoln visited Antietam Battlefield two weeks after the battle and spent four days visiting General George McClellan, touring the battlefield and visiting the wounded of both sides. *An honor, indeed.*

### 15TH MASSACHUSETTS
The 15th Massachusetts Infantry went into the Battle of Antietam with 606 soldiers. 318 were killed or wounded, the highest number for any Union regiment in the battle.

### ARTILLERY HELL!
More than 500 cannons participated in the Battle of Antietam, firing at least 50,000 rounds of ammunition. The cannonade was so severe that Confederate artillery commander Colonel S. D. Lee described the battle as "artillery hell!"

### BLOODBATH
The Battle of Antietam in Maryland was the bloodiest one-day battle in American history. 23,000 soldiers were killed, wounded or missing after 12 hours of savage combat on September 17, 1862. The Battle of Antietam ended the Confederate Army of Northern Virginia's first invasion into the North.

### HOME AT LAST?
Confederate Thomas Tibbs, a lieutenant in the 34th Virginia Infantry, led troops across his family farm during the last battle of Appomattox Court House in Virginia. He fought in the last battle on his own home property, located just beyond the village.

Virginia is named capital of the Confederate States of America...Texas secedes; joins Confederacy...South Carolina troops attack Federal Fort Sumter...Civil War

Party forms to establish black power in America...1967...President Lyndon B. Johnson appoints the first black U.S. Supreme Court Justice, Thurgood Marshall...1968...Dr. Martin Luther King, Jr., is assassinated in Memphis, Tennessee...New

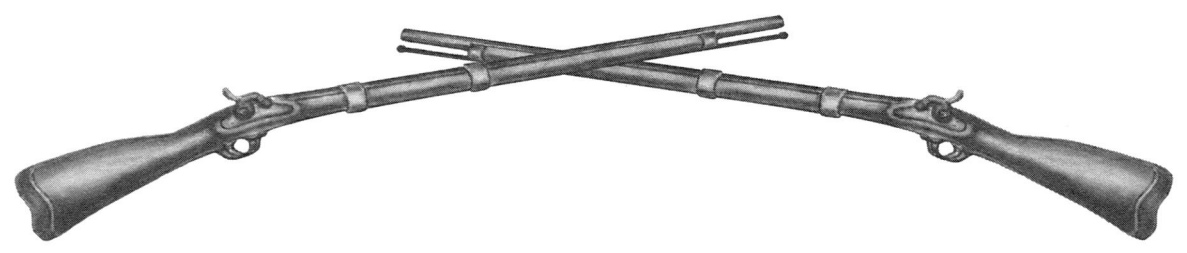

### AFRICAN AMERICAN TROOPS AT APPOMATTOX
Several regiments of United States Colored Troops fought on the front line in the Battle of Appomattox Court House on the morning of April 9, 1865. Several regiments of United States Colored Troops (about 2,000 men) fought on the front line in this battle. Three of these regiments were among the first Federal units to come into the town, and a number of Confederates surrendered to them.

### DON'T HARASS ME!
On April 10, 1865, Generals Lee and Grant met a second time at Appomattox Court House, Virginia. At that second meeting, General Lee requested that his men be given evidence that they were paroled prisoners—to protect them from arrest or harassment. 28,231 parole passes were issued to Confederates.

### LAST BATTLE
In the last battle at Appomattox Court House, fought literally hours before Lee and Grant met for the surrender, nearly 700 men became casualties: killed, wounded, or captured.

Lee surrenders at Appomattox Court House

### AULD LANG SYNE
According to the "History of the 198th Regiment of the Pennsylvania Volunteers," as General Lee left the McLean House *one of our bands, near by, through the generous impulse of the moment, struck up the appropriate air of "Auld Lang Syne."* You know: "Should old acquaintance be forgot…"

### GRANT WEIGHS IN
After the war, there was talk of putting General Lee on trial for treason. Grant wrote, "I will resign the command of the army rather than execute any order to arrest Lee." That settled the matter, and Lee was never tried. *We enemies gotta stick together!*

### BATTLE OF APPOMATTOX REDUX
Two battles were fought at Appomattox before the surrender. On April 8th, Union cavalry attacked Confederate artillery at Appomattox Station. The next morning, Confederate troops attempted to break out, but were halted by Union infantry and cavalry in the Battle of Appomattox Court House.

### A BRIDGE OF UNION
Memorial Bridge was built in 1933 as a symbol of reunification after the Civil War. The bridge crosses the Potomac River, the boundary between North and South during the war. It connects Arlington House (the South) and the Lincoln Memorial (the North), in Washington, D.C.

### THE BIG FOUR!
The four Union generals given credit for bringing an end to the Civil War (General Ulysses S. Grant, William T. Sherman, George H. Thomas, and Philip Sheridan) were all in Chattanooga in the autumn of 1863 to command the Chattanooga Campaign, which the Union forces won, setting the stage for Sherman's march through Georgia.

### LAST SOUTHERN VICTORY
The Battle of Chickamauga, just southeast of Chattanooga, was the last major Confederate victory of the Civil War.

### PLAY BALL!
One of the first photographs taken of the game of baseball was taken at Fort Pulaski in Georgia in 1862. Members of the 48th New York Volunteers stationed at Fort Pulaski played baseball to pass the time. *Today, the Sand Gnats play in Savannah!*

### FORT PULASKI
Fort Pulaski on the coast of Georgia was used as a prison during the Civil War, holding more than 500 Confederate prisoners during the winter of 1864. *It was named for Casimir Pulaski, of Revolutionary War fame.*

### 20 HOURS OF MISERY!
The longest sustained intense fight of the Civil War occurred at the Bloody Angle, a slight bend on the west side of the Mule Shoe at Spotsylvania, Virginia. For up to 20 hours, men were engaged in a hand-to-hand and close-in fight that not even darkness put an end to!

### WE SURRENDER—AGAIN!
Harpers Ferry, the site of John Brown's raid, changed hands eight times during the Civil War. One of the changes was the largest surrender of Federal troops during the Civil War.

### MASON-DIXON LINE
Charles Mason and Jeremiah Dixon surveyed the Mason-Dixon line between 1763 and 1767 to resolve a border dispute between British colonies in Colonial America. The actual survey line forms part of the border of Pennsylvania, Maryland, West Virginia and Delaware. By the 1800s, the line was the northern limit of the slave-owning states and symbolized a cultural boundary between the North and the South. *The term is still used to day to indicate North or South, as in "They drink sweet tea south of the Mason-Dixon line."*

### DIVIDED STATES
Technically, Missouri was a Union state. However, Missouri troops fought on both sides of the war, with more than 100,000 fighting for the Union and nearly 40,000 fighting for the Confederacy. Kentucky was another state where brother literally fought against brother—about 75,000 Kentuckians fought for the Union and 25,000 fought for the Confederacy.

### THE SOUTH BEFORE THE WAR
At the start of the Civil War, the Confederacy had a population of 9 million—5.5 million whites and 3.5 million slaves—with nearly 1.14 million men of combat age. It had 20,000 factories employing nearly 100,000 workers, 9,000 miles of railroad, $47 million in bank deposits, and $37 million in gold. *After the war, all those numbers were greatly reduced!*

### THE NORTH BEFORE THE WAR
The Union states had a population of about 22 million before the war, with 4 million men of combat age. It had 100,000 factories employing more than 1 million workers, 20,000 miles of railroad, 96% of the combined nations' railroad equipment, the majority of coal mines and canals, $189 million in bank deposits, and $56 million in gold.

Bull Run—first official battle of the Civil War…1862…1st ironclad ship battle between Monitor and Merrimac…2nd Battle of Bull Run ends in Union defeat

in a political trial in California… Equal Employment Opportunity Act passes…1974…The Coalition of Labor Union Women is formed…1978…U.S. Postal Service issues a Black Heritage postage stamp series…1983…Martin Luther King, Jr. Day is

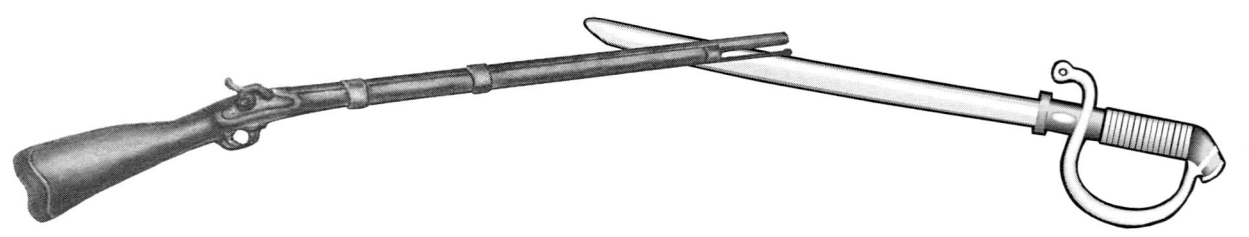

### THE POPULATION GROWS
In the five years between 1861 and 1865, 800,000 Europeans—mainly English, Irish, and Germans—immigrated to America despite the Civil War. Most growth was in the North since immigrants entered the country in New York. A lot of immigrants fought for the North during the war, mostly Irish and German.

### A TREND?
Abraham Lincoln was the first American president to wear a beard! *Though one little girl wrote him a letter saying he would look better without it; he shaved, and won the election!*

### DIXIE REDUX
"Dixie" was such a popular song in the 1860s that it was played at the inaugurations of both Abraham Lincoln and Jefferson Davis. *Which just goes to show a great tune trumps war anytime.*

### FIGHTING FORCES
Approximately 80% of the Union fighting forces was infantry, 14% cavalry, and 6% artillery. The Confederate Army had a similar proportion of artillery but a slightly higher proportion of cavalry. *Would you have wanted to be a walker or a rider?*

### PORTRAIT OF A UNION SOLDIER
The Union Army consisted of approximately 2.2 million men. They ranged in age from 18-46, the average age being in the mid-twenties. The majority had been farmers, and very few had any previous military experience. The average Union soldier was 5 feet 8 inches tall and weighed 145 pounds. About 75% were born in the United States, and nearly all were volunteers.

### GRANT'S FORCES
In the six weeks from the Battle of the Wilderness on May 4, 1864 to the beginning of the siege of Petersburg, casualties to Grant's forces ran as high as 60,000-70,000 men. Although Grant made up the losses with replacements, the toll appalled the North and Grant was heavily criticized.

### SHERMAN'S NECKTIES
General Sherman's men burned many homes in their paths, generally leaving nothing standing except the masonry chimneys. These became known as "Sherman Sentinels." Railroad ties that the soldiers heated and then wrapped around trees became know as "Sherman's Neckties." Such destruction was done to disable the railroads and make it impossible to do any quick repairs!

### AWOL!
By the late fall of 1864, morale was very low among Confederate troops. Confederate records are pretty sketchy, but it's believed that 100,000-200,000 enlisted soldiers did not report for duty! *AWOL= Absent Without Leave, a real no-no in the military, then and now.*

### WE NEED EVERYONE!
During the siege of Petersburg, the Confederate army was so desperate for able bodies to man its defenses that it resorted to using old men, young boys, and two unwilling members of Jefferson Davis's cabinet! *But did they bring their desks?*

### TOTAL CASUALTIES
Total Confederate and Union deaths attributed to the Civil War from both battle and disease is approximately 623,000. At least 471,400 more were wounded. The total casualty list for the war is about 1,094,400.

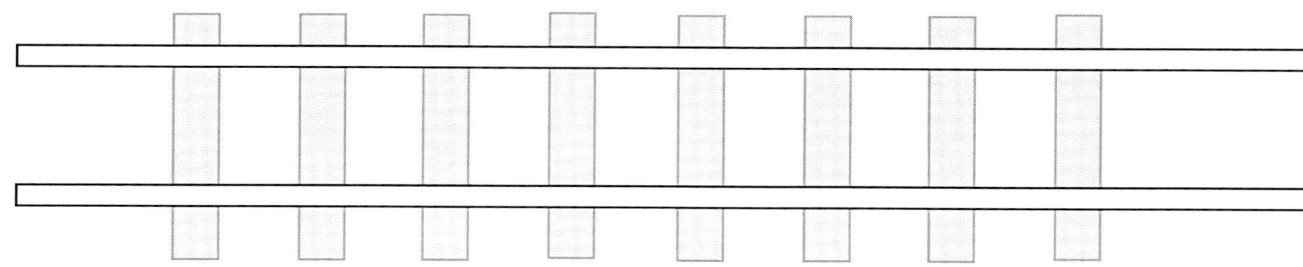

### CIVIL WAR NAVIES
At the beginning of the war, the U. S. Navy had 90 ships. During the war, it built 208 and bought 418 more. The Confederates had no ships but managed to buy, convert, or build about 500 vessels of all sorts for use during the war.

### THE BLOCKADE
As the war progressed, the Union blockade of Southern ports became more effective. In 1861, at the beginning of the war, only one in ten blockade runners was captured. By 1864, that number had risen to one in three.

### ACTION FOR THE NAVY
There was a naval action at sea nearly every day of the war. Southern blockade runners tried to evade Union blockading ships, and chases and captures kept the Union navy busy. The number of attempted violations of the blockade is said to be about 8,200.

### CAPTURE OF NEW ORLEANS
Union officer David Farragut sailed his fleet into New Orleans on April 25, 1862, and captured the city with little resistance. By taking New Orleans, located 100 miles above the mouth of the Mississippi River, the Union effectively controlled the gateway to the Deep South.

### THE JAMES BROTHERS
Frank and Jesse James began their lives of violence as Confederate guerrillas during the Civil War. They roamed Missouri wreaking havoc on Union forces and Northern sympathizers. After the war, the James brothers turned to a life of crime. *As we well know!*

### FLORIDA AT WAR
Approximately 14,000 Floridians fought for the Confederacy and about 2,000 for the Union. About 5,000 Floridian soldiers died during the war.

### THE BATTLE OF OLUSTEE
The Battle of Olustee in northern Florida was one of the bloodiest Civil War battles in terms of the percentage of casualties—3,000 of the 10,000 soldiers there were dead, wounded, or missing by the battle's end.

### BLACK MARKET
Petersburg, Virginia, was linked to Wilmington, North Carolina by the Petersburg and Weldon Railroad. Wilmington was the Confederacy's chief destination for Confederate blockade runners loaded with European goods and supplies for citizens and soldiers alike. *The "black market" was the illegal sale of goods.*

### FIRST AID FOR PETERSBURG
Slaves who entered Union lines and came to City Point, Virginia (present day Hopewell) during the Siege of Petersburg, were typically employed unloading ships and working in hospitals. The Depot Field Hospital, which was located in City Point, Virginia, was the largest field hospital for Union or Southern troops during the Civil War. The Confederate government hired slaves from the Richmond vicinity and employed them in the construction of fortifications protecting the capital city.

### CONFEDERATES—GONE! (BUT NOT FORGOTTEN!)
No Union troops, other than prisoners, reached Richmond until after the Confederate government evacuated the city on April 2, 1865.

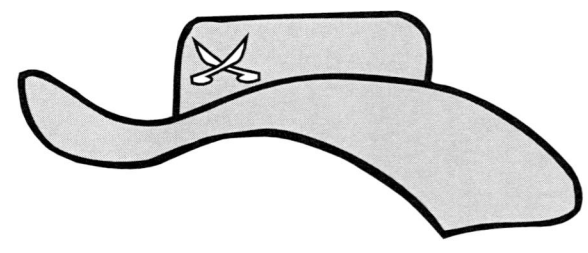

### THE BIG BANG!
The artillery firing at Malvern Hill, Pennsylvania was so loud that people living 100 miles away claimed to have heard it!

### DAVIS UNDER FIRE

During the 1862 battles before Richmond, Confederate President Jefferson Davis personally visited several of the battlefields, at times coming under enemy fire. He saw action at Seven Pines, Beaver Dam Creek, Glendale, and Malvern Hill.

### PATIENT OVERLOAD!
Between 1861 and 1865, Chimborazo Hospital in Richmond, Virginia treated approximately 75,000 patients, more than any other facility in either the North or South! *Take a number!*

### TOURING THE TROOPS
President Abraham Lincoln visited the Richmond area twice during the war. In July 1862, he met with General McClellan at Harrison's Landing on the James River. Lincoln came to Richmond on April 4, 1865 and walked the streets of a city still smoldering from the evacuation fire.

### SMALL ARMS AND THE SOLDIER
Small arms are the weapons that soldiers carried on them. The most common small arms weapons used during the Civil War included:
- Musket—an infantryman's light gun with a long barrel, typically smooth-bored, muzzle-loading, and fired from the shoulder.
- Rifle—a gun fired from shoulder level, having a long spirally-grooved barrel intended to make a bullet spin, which produced greater accuracy over a long distance.
- Carbine—a light, short-barreled rifle, commonly used by the cavalry.
- Handgun—a gun designed to be fired with one hand, usually either a pistol or revolver.

### UNION GUNS!
When the war began, the Union had more than 400,000 rifles and muskets stored in the Federal arsenal. With the weapons brought by state militia, they thought this would be more than enough to bring the Southern rebellion under control. Within *only a few weeks*, all the guns were given out and the Rebels weren't even close to quitting the fight!

### CONFEDERATE GUNS!
The Confederacy had even fewer guns than the Union at the start of the war—only 296,000 shoulder arms, most of them outdated flintlock muskets, in their arsenal. There were only 24,000 modern rifles to distribute to the troops. The Confederacy asked for gun donations from private people and relied on capturing Federal arsenals once the war began. *Whatever works?*

### FIREPOWER AND LOTS OF IT!
According to a Union munitions expert, it required 140 pounds of powder and 900 pounds of lead to kill each Confederate who was shot on the battlefield. It seems that weapons fire was often wildly inaccurate due to the limitations of the weapons and the panic of the men in battle. Some soldiers estimated it took a man's weight in lead to kill a single enemy!

### SWORDS AND SABERS
Very plain swords were issued to Union sergeants, cavalrymen, select artillerymen, and musicians. They were expected to be used for fighting rather than for dress. Swords issued to officers were much 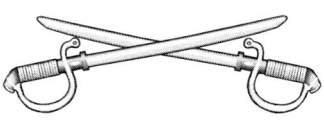 more ornate and served more as a symbol of rank. Only the sabers carried by cavalry and light artillery officers were actual weapons, though they weren't used as often as rifles and sidearms.

...Union gains control of Mississippi River...West Virginia joins Union as free state...Battle of Gettysburg begins to turn tide of war for Union... Lincoln gives

Condoleezza Rice to serve as his U.S. National Security Advisor...2002...Tiger Woods becomes the youngest golfer (age 26!) to win 8 PGA major titles.. African American tennis star Serena Williams wins the U.S. Open and Wimbledon

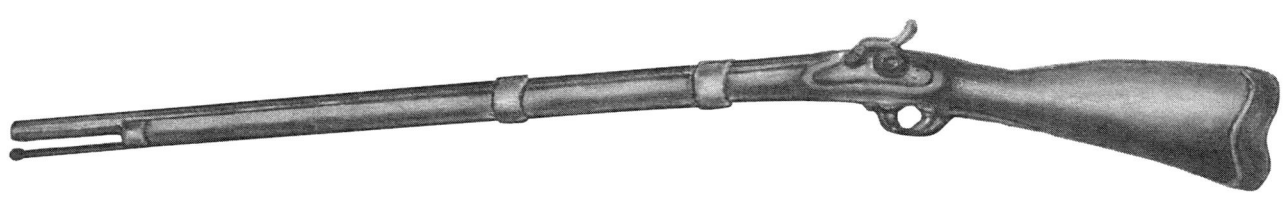

### ON GUARD!
Swords appealed to Confederate soldiers more than Union soldiers because swords symbolized an era of romance and chivalry, which was still popular in the South at that time. As with the Union, swords were both a symbol of rank and a fighting weapon, but they were rarely used.

### CANNONS AND CANNONBALLS!
The most commonly used artillery for both the Union and the Confederacy was the Napoleon, a smoothbore, muzzle-loaded howitzer whose projectile weighed 12 pounds! Its maximum range was 1,000 yards, but the weapon was most effective at 250 yards or less. It used canister ammunition and grape shot and is believed to have killed more men on both sides than all other artillery weapons combined! *Nothing "boring" about that!*

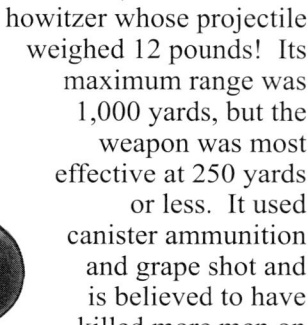

### FIRING A CANNON
Firing a cannon required a well-coordinated routine by several soldiers. Experienced gunners could load and fire a fieldpiece every 30 seconds—even in the face of enemy fire! Gunnery teams were a close-knit bunch who treated their weapons as members of the family, often giving them special names!

### HORSE ARTILLERY
Horse artillery was the name given to small but powerful cannons that could be taken apart, packed onto horses, and carried over rough terrain. Cavalry commonly used horse artillery, and Confederate generals Jeb Stuart and Nathan Forrest put it to excellent use in the Civil War.

### PLAY ON!
Both sides of the conflict had bands that would play in the evening. In 1861, a count showed that 75% of all Union regiments had a band. Most bands were disbanded by mid-July 1862, though, because they were too expensive. *So the music didn't play on, but war music was popular then, and still today!*

### PAYDAY!
Top pay for a Union infantry private was $16 a month. For a Confederate, it was $18 a month—but it was worth considerably less than the Union private's pay because of skyrocketing inflation!

### WHERE HAVE YOU FOUGHT?
Beginning in the winter of 1861-62, Union troops began marking their national and regimental flags with the names of the battles in which they had fought. This was a practice that went back to the 1830s in the regular army.

### FIRE!
Many times wounded soldiers perished in raging brushfires that were ignited during heavy gunfire in dry fields and forests. A number of battles were temporarily halted while both sides struggled to save their wounded from brushfires that threatened to engulf them!

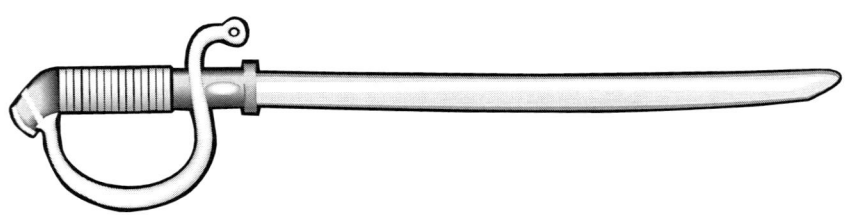

### SNIPERS
Both sides used sharpshooters to pick off the enemy at a great distance. At the Battle of Spotsylvania, one Confederate sniper shot a Union general dead at 800 yards! (That's more than the length of six football fields!)

### UNION POW CAMPS
• Point Lookout in Maryland was designed to house 10,000 men in tents, but often contained 20,000 or more.
• Fort Jefferson in the Dry Tortugas, off the Florida Keys, was known for its brutal conditions. The old fort, converted into a military prison in 1861, housed Union army criminals who often died from the tropical heat and unsanitary conditions.
• The worst Union POW camp was located in Elmira, New York. More than 2,960 Confederate prisoners—nearly a quarter of the prison population—died there from disease, starvation, filthy living conditions, and freezing to death. Many who survived the camp called it "Hellmira."

### FORT JEFFERSON
This prison's most famous prisoner was Dr. Samuel Mudd, who set John Wilkes Booth's broken leg following the assassination of Abraham Lincoln. Mudd claimed he hadn't recognized Booth when he set his leg, but he was sentenced to life in prison. President Andrew Jackson pardoned and released him in 1869.

### ANDERSONVILLE, AGAIN
The South's most notorious prison camp was Andersonville in Sumter County, Georgia. Opened in 1864, it was designed to house 10,000 men but soon had more than 3 times that number. With little food, no fresh water, inadequate shelter from the blistering heat or cold, no clothing or medical attention, about 13,000 prisoners died there—a mortality rate of about 29%.

### A SMALL CITY
At its maximum, Andersonville had more than 33,000 Union prisoners, making it the 5th largest city in the Confederacy. As Union armies neared Atlanta, 100 miles north, Confederates worried that a cavalry raid might free the prisoners and form an army at the Confederate rear.

### AMPUTATIONS!
The treatment of choice for a soldier's broken or lacerated limbs was immediate amputation. Patients were anesthetized with chloroform, ether, nitrous oxide, or at least a glass of whiskey! When no anesthesia was available, several strong orderlies would hold the patient down, and someone would place a cloth or bullet in his mouth for him to bite on while the doctor attended to him with a knife and saw. One famous Civil War photograph shows a stack of amputated arms and legs as high as a haystack!

### AND THEY'RE OFF!
An experienced field doctor could amputate a leg with a knife and saw in two minutes. In a large battle, a doctor would work nonstop for hours and there was often a grisly pile of severed limbs stacked like cordwood beside the operating table. According to U. S. Army records, only about 7,000 of the nearly 29,000 amputations performed resulted in death. The most successful were the surgeries performed within 48 hours of injury. However, infections at the wound often later killed soldiers. Little was known about germs and doctors would go from patient to patient without washing their hands, use the same tools on each patient, and other things that we know today were highly unsanitary.

...Maryland abolishes slavery...Nevada joins union as free state...Abraham Lincoln wins reelection as president...Sherman begins "March to the Sea" through

Coordinating Committee, led by prominent African American lawyers and activists, announce plans to sue companies that profited from slavery... President George W. Bush awards comedian and actor Bill Cosby and baseball player Hank Aaron

### CHILDREN SOLDIERS
According to U. S. military records:
- 127 Union soldiers were 13 years old when they enlisted;
- 320 soldiers were 14 years old;
- Nearly 800 were 15 years old;
- 2,758 were 16 years old;
- And about 6,500 were 17 years old;
- There are no numbers regarding the ages of underage solders in the South, but historians believe the numbers were higher.

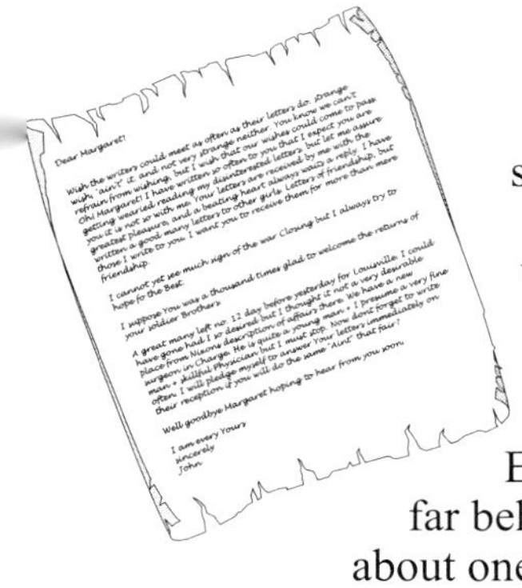

### CIVIL WAR LETTERS
Today, a handwritten letter from a soldier in the field during the Civil War can sell for hundreds or even thousands of dollars at an auction. *Check grandma's attic!*

### EDUCATION IN THE SOUTH
Education for Southern whites was far behind Northern standards. In 1860, about one in five Southern white men were illiterate, while the illiteracy rate for Southern white women was much higher. Slaves were seldom taught to read and write.

### SOUTHERN RURAL LIFE
There were far more small and midsize farms in the South than there were plantations—and most were tended without slaves. This is the opposite of the impression often given of Southern rural life at the start of the Civil War.

### PLANTATION LIFE
A working plantation was usually made up of a large family home, slave quarters, smokehouses, gardens, a stockyard, and the farmland itself, which could be hundreds, or thousands, of acres. Most large plantations were fairly self-sufficient. Most plantations grew cotton, tobacco, indigo, and/or rice. Slaves worked in the field, and occasionally so did paid white laborers. In a good year, each field slave produced a profit of $250.

### WE'RE LEAVING!
General Robert E. Lee urged Southerners to remain in the United States and make lives as good citizens after the war. But it's estimated that 10,000-20,000 Confederates left rather than live under the U. S. government! Where did they go? Some to the Western Territory at that time which had little government control, and others to Mexico, Canada, and South America.

### SLAVERY ABOLISHED!
Slavery was not officially abolished until after the Civil War, when the 13th Amendment to the U.S. Constitution was ratified at the end of 1865. Only three-fourths of the states were needed to ratify the 13th Amendment. Some states rejected it at the time. Kentucky ratified it in 1976, but Mississippi didn't get around to it until 1995! *The wheels of progress often move slowly!*

### RECONSTRUCTION
After the Civil War, the defeated South was a ruined land. Invading Union forces had inflicted enormous destruction. The old social, economic, and political order that was founded on slavery had collapsed completely. During the period between 1865 and 1877 known as Reconstruction, the federal government controlled the Confederacy in an attempt to rebuild the region as well as restore the relationship between the Southern states and the federal government.

Georgia…1865…Robert E. Lee appointed general-in-chief of all Confederate armies…Missouri abolishes slavery…Abraham Lincoln rejects Jefferson Davis's

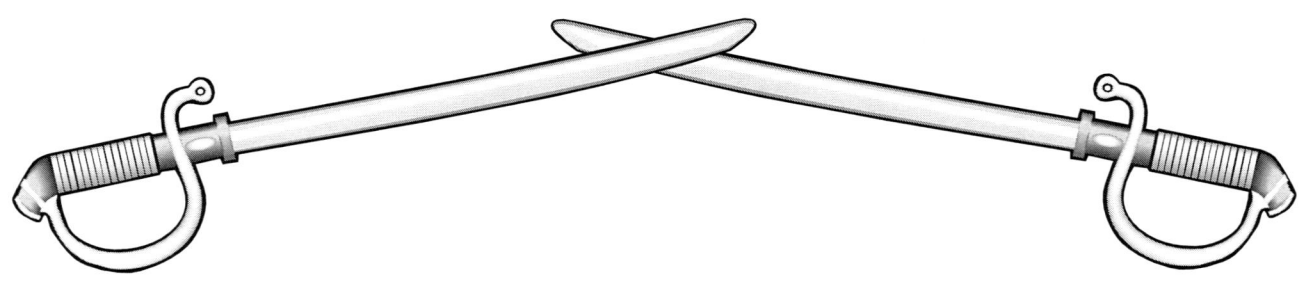

### THE FREEDMEN'S BUREAU
During Reconstruction, the Union assumed responsibility for newly freed slaves. In 1865, Congress established the Bureau of Refugees, Freedmen, and Abandoned Lands, which became known as the Freedmen's Bureau. The bureau helped provide food, housing, medical and dental care. It trained teachers and assisted in building more than 1,000 schools and colleges. The bureau helped former slaves for seven years until it was discontinued in 1872, due to lack of proper funding.

### THE END OF RECONSTRUCTION
Reconstruction ended in 1877 when the Republicans agreed to withdraw Federal soldiers from the South in exchange for Southern support for contested electoral votes for Rutherford B. Hayes. Hayes became the 19th president of the United States and Reconstruction ended.

### *GONE WITH THE WIND*
Atlanta author Margaret Mitchell won a Pulitzer Prize for her 1937 novel *Gone With the Wind*. Mitchell told the story of Scarlett O'Hara, a strong-willed Southern woman who survives the Civil War and Reconstruction. The book has sold tens of millions of copies, but is criticized today because of its romantic view of the South and its demeaning depiction of African Americans, both as slaves and as freed persons.

### BLOCKHOUSES
Blockhouses were small, simple log buildings built in small garrisons to protect soldiers from enemy attacks. They had small openings in the walls from which to fire a rifle at the enemy.

### THAT LOUSE WINS EVERY TIME
Lice was unavoidable for Civil War soldiers, but one way to turn annoying lice into entertainment was to race them! Soldiers picked their lice, put them on plates, and held races to see which one could cross the plate first! One story goes that the lice of one particular soldier was always winning and no one could figure out why. His friends finally found out that he got his lice to run across the play faster by heating the plate right before the race began! *It's hard to beat a hot-footed louse!*

### BREASTWORKS
Breastworks were generally built just before a battle, usually using dirt accumulated from digging trenches. Soldiers used dirt and anything else that would help give protection from the enemy. The name breastworks comes from the fact that the fortifications were about breast high. *Good to know…*

### FORTS
Forts were permanent fortifications built at strategic locations. In addition to walls and a battery of guns to protect the soldiers, forts also enclosed many buildings, including barracks for sleeping, kitchens for preparing food and eating, and storage areas for food, supplies, ammunition and guns.

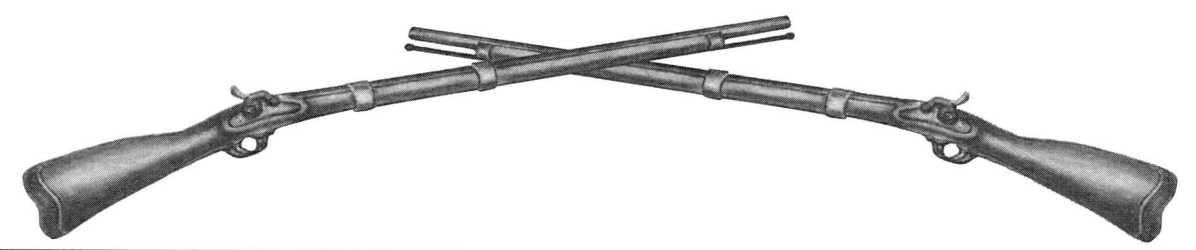

### BATTERIES
Soldiers would set up a battery, or group, of guns on the walls of a fort to protect against enemy attack.

### TRANSPORTATION
Mostly, Civil War soldiers got from one place to another by marching. Officers and cavalry rode horses, but most everyone else walked. Supplies and large equipment, such as cannons, were moved using horses and wagons. Ships and trains also came into play during the Civil War, but on a limited basis and only for transporting troops and equipment long distances. At this time, steam was used to power both ships and trains.

### SMILE, PLEASE!
Photography was fairly new at the time of the Civil War. Cameras were much larger than they are today and moving them from one place to another was not an easy task. In fact, the entire process was a slow and complex process. Often, both newspaper and army photographers followed armies into battle to get pictures of the battle scene. *And yes, they were in harm's way!*

### EXTRA! EXTRA!!
Newspaper reporters traveled by horse and wagon to cover the war. The reporters sent stories back to their newspapers to be published and they also brought news to the soldiers. Before photography, artists would sketch pictures of a battlefield for newspapers and magazines.

### UP!
Hot air balloons, or observation balloons, were sometimes used to report troop movements and battles.

### HOSPITALS TO GO
Portable hospitals were usually tents set up near battlefields to look after sick and injured soldiers. Armies also had no problem taking over a civilian home or barn near a battlefield to be used as a hospital.

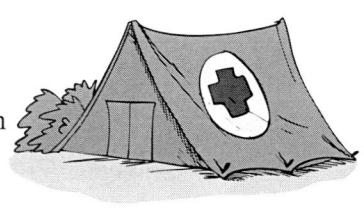

### AMBULANCE WAGONS
Designated "ambulance wagons" were used to care for and transport injured soldiers from the battlefield to the nearest hospital.

### FINAL CIVIL WAR STATS
The Civil War consisted of more than 50 major battles and 5,000 minor battles. More than 360,000 Union soldiers and 260,000 Confederate soldiers died and many, many more were wounded. In addition, as many as 100,000 civilians died. Just about every family had someone in the war, and 1 in 4 soldiers were killed. Many others came home, but were never the same due to severe injuries or psychological trauma.

### EXACTLY FOUR YEARS—ALMOST!
The American Civil War began on April 12, 1861, at Fort Sumter, South Carolina, and ended on April 9, 1865, at Appomattox Court House, Virginia—almost exactly four years to the day it started!

### EXTRA, EXTRA, READ ALL ABOUT IT!
Interest in the Civil War never goes away! *The Civil War News* is a monthly publication with news, book reviews, and a calendar of past Civil War events as well as current activities. Learn more at www.civilwarnews.com.

### WRAP UP IN A CIVIL WAR BLANKET
The Amana Woolen Mill in Iowa, which has been operating since 1857 (before the Civil War began!), makes a Civil War wool blanket just like the ones soldiers carried. It is striped and comes in several colors. The company made 170 of the blankets to be used as props in the "Andersonville" mini-series aired on Turner Television Network in 1996. amanawoolenmill.com.

### LEE'S EYES AND EARS
General Robert E. Lee called his cavalry general, JEB Stuart, "his eyes and his ears." JEB are Stuart's initials – James Ewell Brown Stuart.

### LAST CONFEDERATE GENERAL
The last surviving Confederate general, Simon Bolivar Buckner, died in 1914, at the age of 91.

### WE SURRENDER!
Nashville, Tennessee was the first state capital of the Confederacy to fall to Union troops. It happened in 1862, less than a year after the war began.

### TERMS OF SURRENDER
General Lee agreed to terms that said that all Confederate soldiers who owned their own horses could keep them, and all Confederate officers could keep their sidearms and swords.

### THE KEY
The Civil War Tomb of the Unknown Dead, in Arlington Cemetery in Washington, D.C., was dedicated in 1866. It contains the remains of 2,111 unidentified Union and Confederate soldiers. The tomb is located on the site of the former Custis and Lee family flower garden. A large brass key to the tomb is on display at the historic Arlington House, the former home of Robert E. Lee and his wife, Mary Custis Lee.

## Good Civil War Books for young readers...

*Civil War Ghost Stories & Legends*
Nancy Roberts

*Civil War Heroines*
Bellerophon Books

*Book of the American Civil War*
Brown, Little & Co.

*Civil War Trivia*
Edward F. Williams III

*The Civil War: Strange & Fascinating Facts*
Burke Davis

*Dogs of War: And Stories of Other Beasts of Battle in the Civil War*
Marilyn Seguin

*The Red Badge of Courage*
Stephen Crane

*Escape To Freedom: The Underground Railroad Adventures Of Callie And William*
Barbara Brooks Simon

*Rousing Songs & True Tales of the Civil War*
Wayne Erbsen

*Civil War Book of Facts*
Frank Burd

*Flags of the Confederacy*
Ray DiZazzo

Andrew Johnson sworn into office...John Wilkes Booth shot and killed in Bowling Green, Virginia...President Johnson submits plan for Restoration of South

Africa... 2008... Barack Obama wins presidential election becoming first African American president-elect... 2009... Barack Obama is inaugurated as the first African American President ...Michelle Obama is the first African American First Lady...

# Reconstruction

*Reconstruction: the recovery and rebuilding period following the Civil War*

> Can you believe the war is finally over? The weight of the world has been lifted from my husband's shoulders. I can see it in his eyes. And we are going to Ford's Theatre to see a play tonight! A night of lighthearted fun—I cannot wait!—**Mary Todd Lincoln**

> POP! What was that? Part of the play? Women are shrieking! A man has leaped onto the stage, yelled, and run off. The president slumps in his chair! I see blood! Can it be true?! Did someone just shoot our president?!—**usher**, Ford's Theatre

> *Stop that man!*—**Major Henry Rathbone**

> Everyone is sobbing. Our president died early this morning. May God have mercy on this country.—**newspaper reporter**

> I accept this office of President of the United States with a heavy heart.—Vice President **Andrew Johnson**

**Lincoln Shot!**

> He was in that barn and wouldn't come out. So we set it on fire! I saw my chance, and took it. I shot him. I shot and killed that John Wilkes Booth.—**Union soldier** *

*The manhunt for John Wilkes Booth was the largest in history, involving 10,000 federal troops, detectives, and police.

### The Legend of *Taps*

In 1862, Union Army Captain Robert Ellicombe looked over the battle scene. He heard the groan of a wounded soldier. Although, he did not know if the soldier was a Union soldier or a Confederate soldier, the captain crawled through the battle amidst gunfire and carried the soldier to the medical tent. When he got back, he found that the soldier was a Confederate, but he was already dead. He recognized the face of the soldier and realized it was his own son. Because the son was a Rebel, he was not allowed to have a full military burial. Only one musician, a bugler, was allowed to play. The father asked the bugler to play a song that was found in the pocket of his son's uniform. The bugler played the song that became known as *Taps*.

**This story is legend, not historically accurate**

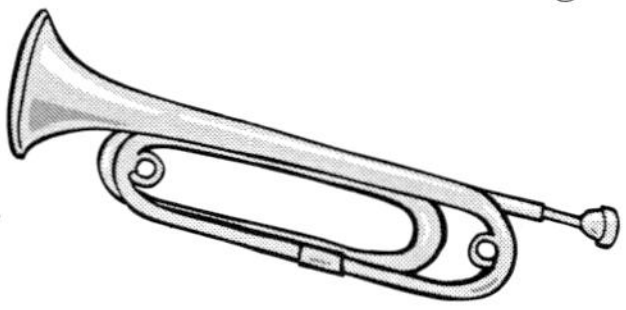

### The True Story of *Taps*

General Daniel Butterfield was dissatisfied with the customary firing of three rifles at the end of military burials. He altered a French bugle call into what is now known as *Taps*. The song became very popular, and within months it was sounded by both the Union and Confederate armies.

**This story is the true story of *Taps*. Not as fun and romantic as the Legend!**

> Here are the latest statistics, Sir: 618,000 soldiers dead; probably 100,000 civilians killed too, Sir. That includes the North and South, Sir. And we know that disease killed twice as many as those who died in battle.—**Union soldier** *

*The Civil War death toll is more than the total killed in battle in the American Revolution, War of 1812, Mexican War, Spanish-American War, World War I, World War II, Korean War, Vietnam, and Gulf War—all combined!

> When we said our vows years ago, I was just a child. Jefferson was 18 years my elder. My momma almost cried when I said I wanted to marry him. But we've had a happy life together. Full of struggles, I suppose, but happy. I never thought I'd be the First Lady of the Confederacy, not in a million years! But I stand by Jefferson in everything. Right now he's locked up, accused of treason since the great South lost this Civil War. But I'm staying right here outside his jail cell. I'll fight for his release until I feel him back in my arms again, no matter how long it takes.—**Varina Howell Davis***

*Jefferson Davis was released in 1867 thanks to his wife's unrelenting requests for his freedom.

> Everything is destroyed! Houses burned. Fields barren. Animals dead or dying—I can count their ribs. What has happened to our beautiful South?—**Confederate soldier**

> My lifeless body hangs on the scaffold. Three guilty men wave in the wind beside me. They accused me of conspiring to kill Abraham Lincoln. I did no such thing!—ghost of **Mary Surratt**

> If these old walls could talk, they would tell a history so fascinating and terrifying, no student would ever tire of learning about American events. I was built years ago, before any of these men were even born. My walls were erected for protection, but just look at them now. Spirits seem to haunt this sad and forlorn place, and will forever more.—**Fort Monroe**

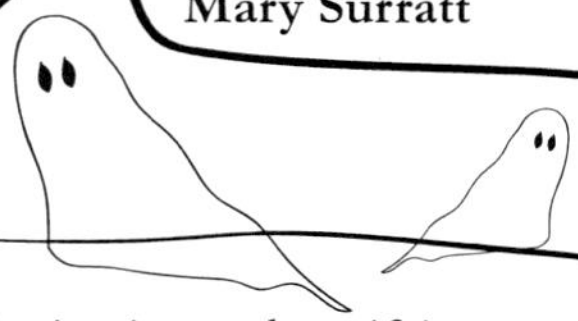

...All Confederate states except Mississippi readmitted to Union...Six Confederate officers form anti-black society, Ku Klux Klan...1866...Congress passes Civil

Susan Rice is the first African American woman to become the United States' U.N. Ambassador... Eric Holder is the first African American Attorney General of the United States... 50-year-old pop icon Michael Jackson dies of cardiac arres t...Venus

Did I ever think I would see this day? No, sir! No more slavery—thanks to the Thirteenth Amendment to the Constitution. What a day, what a day! Free at last! Praise the Lord!—**former slave**

We've got to keep these free blacks under control! We'll wear white robes and hoods and terrorize them at night—they'll think we're spirits of Confederate soldiers! That'll keep them in their place.—**Ku Klux Klan member**\*

\* The Ku Klux Klan was a secret society organized by Southerners that used violence and terror to maintain "white supremacy."

I thought the war was over! But they passed that Military Reconstruction Act and Union troops are still here—occupying the South! It's like pouring salt into a fresh wound. And those Northerners wonder why we're bitter?!—**Southern schoolteacher**

Carpetbaggers! Scalawags! Just look at them taking advantage of our pain to make money for themselves! Why, if one of them comes into my shop, I'll shoo him out so fast his hat will spin right off his head!—**Southern shopkeeper**

Thank ya, suh for these clothes to wear and food for my fam'ly. We have nothin'. Don't know what we'd do without the Freedman's Bureau to help us. It seems like everyone else is ag'in us.—**freed slave**\*

\*The Freedman's Bureau was a federal agency formed to help former slaves get food, clothing, medical care, and fair treatment after the war.

Tenants ain't got no chance. I don't know who gets the money, but it ain't the poor. It gets worse every year—the land gets more wore out, the price for tobacco gets lower, and everything you got to buy gets higher. Like I said, I'm trying to 'be content' like the Bible says and not to worry, but I don't see no hope.—**sharecropper's wife**

We have great hopes for the Fourteenth Amendment! It grants equality to all citizens, but big problems still exist between blacks and whites in the South. Southern states have passed Black Codes—laws to deny former slaves their rights. There is still such violence…will they ever embrace each other?—**Northern Congressman**

So far from engaging in a war to perpetuate slavery, I am rejoiced that slavery is abolished. I believe it will be greatly for the interest of the South. So fully am I satisfied of this that I would have cheerfully lost all that I have lost by the war and have suffered all that I have suffered to have this object obtained.—**Robert E. Lee**\*

\*Robert E. Lee spent the rest of his life as President of Washington and Lee University in Lexington, Virginia

I cannot help but feel sad and depressed…at the downfall of a foe who fought so long and valiantly, and had suffered so much for a cause, though that cause was, I believe, one of the worst for which people ever fought.—**Ulysses S. Grant**

Today, I have been elected to the United States Senate! I'm the first black man elected to the U.S. Senate! I must work to protect the rights of my black brethren. They have a steep hill to climb.—**Hiram Revels**, Mississippi

I'll be the first black man to cast my vote after the Fifteenth Amendment grants blacks the right to vote. My parents were slaves…and here I am! What a privilege! What an honor! I can't wait to vote!—**Thomas Mundy Peterson**

*Human nature will not change. In any future great national trial, compared with the men of this, we shall have as weak and as strong, as silly and as wise, as bad and as good. Let us therefore study the incidents of this, as philosophy to learn wisdom from.*— Abraham Lincoln

Think maybe the South could win next time?

We lost?!

g'night John Boy
g'night Mama
g'night Tecumseh
g'night Robert E.
g'night Stonewall
g'…
Lights out, boys!

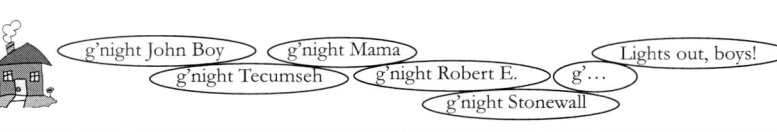

Rights Act…1868…14th Amendment to the Constitution guarantees equal rights…1870…15th Amendment grants blacks right to vote.

and Serena Williams are the first African American world doubles tennis champions…Disney unveils The Princess and the Frog, the studio's first animated film featuring an African American princess.